Cycling
Sussex

Adam Trimingham

Cover design, maps and illustrations by
Tony Ashton Graphic Design & Illustration.

The maps for the 12 rides through Sussex are reproduced
from the Ordnance Survey map by permission of Ordnance
Survey on behalf of the Controller of Her Majesty's
Stationery Office, © Crown Copyright MC 100034502

Published by Pomegranate Press,
Dolphin House, 51 St Nicholas Lane, Lewes, Sussex BN7 2JZ
Email: sussexbooks@compuserve.com

ISBN 09533493-9-X
British Library Cataloguing-in-Publication Data.
A catalogue record of this book is available from the British
Library

Printed by VIP Ltd, The VIP Centre, Ghyll Road, Heathfield,
Sussex TN21 8AW Tel: 01435 861251

Contents

"There are more bikes than cars in this country but you'd never think it looking at the average English road, especially on a wet and windy day. The other morning I seemed to be the only cyclist on the coast road in Brighton – and even the rain was driving"

The joys of cycling Sussex

I'm probably preaching to the converted in claiming that Sussex is one of the best counties in Britain, but you may not have realised that it's one of the finest counties for cycling, too. It's big enough to get lost in occasionally but small enough never to be too far from civilisation. That in cycling terms usually means a pub, a cafe or a shop where you can stoke up.

Even in the biggest town, which is Brighton, you can see bits of the countryside from much of the centre, and you are never more than three or four miles away from green hills. In many of the smaller towns, such as Billingshurst or Crowborough, you can be out in a matter of minutes.

The towns, ranging from the Georgian swank of Chichester to the post-war clean-cut lines of Crawley, contain plenty of interest. The villages number among them several, such as Lindfield, Cuckfield and Ditchling, which are justly famous well beyond their bounds.

The countryside contains amazing variety for a county

Beautiful Lindfield pond.

which is only about 80 miles long and barely 25 from south to north: the coastal plain, wide and flat in the west at Selsey but tapering to a point at Black Rock in east Brighton; the eerie marshes of Pevensey and the bleak countryside east of Hastings, where Sussex merges almost imperceptibly with Kent; the splendid heathland of the Ashdown Forest, matched by many smaller outcrops in sundry parts of Sussex.

The lush pastures of the Low Weald and the surprisingly steep slopes of the High Weald contain many of the great gardens of England such as Sheffield Park, Leonardslee,

Nymans and High Beeches. In the north-western corner is the highest spot of all, Black Down, which is approaching 1,000 feet. Over in the north-east there are hill towns such as Crowborough,while the best rocks in the south east are to be found at Groombridge.

But the dominant feature of the landscape is the chalky South Downs, which rush in from the west near Petersfield and plunge dramatically into the sea at Beachy Head. They are justly celebrated in verse by great Sussex poets such as Kipling and Belloc. Although small compared with the mountains of the north, they are sharply defined and immensely impressive.

You can cycle across most of these landscapes in a single day if you are reasonably fit, but even a more modest rider can see a great range of scenery within ten or twenty miles – as demonstrated by the rides later on in this book.

Cycle up Ditchling Beacon, reaching the summit at 813 feet, and you will be a hero for having reached the highest point on the East Sussex Downs. But there are steeper, if shorter, hills elsewhere which would test a Tour de France rider. You can, on the other hand, ride for miles around Chichester Harbour and climb nothing steeper than a canal bridge.

You can ride everywhere except for the M23 and through a couple of

Ditchling Beacon.

tunnels (but you wouldn't want use those anyway). Most of the busy trunk roads such as the A27 and A23 were once dangerous but now have cycle lanes or tracks along part of their length.

But it's best to ride off these highways if possible, and then you are spoilt for choice. There are thousands of miles of small country roads and lanes, and hundreds of miles of tracks and bridleways where no cars are allowed at all.

You can be alone in the stillness of a wood or high on a hill with

Along the South Downs Way.

only larks for company, and yet you can be home, or at a station on the way, within half an hour.

It's a truly delightful bike-sized county. We're lucky to live in it – and even more fortunate to be pedalling quietly within it.

Keeping fit

There are few better ways of keeping fit than riding a bike. At one extreme you have riders in races such as the Tour de France, one of the most gruelling sporting events in the world. At the other you have someone cycling slowly on a journey along a flat road of three-quarters of a mile to the shops.

Cycling is fairly easy along the flat on a decent bike. It is harder up hills or against the wind, but with good gears it should be possible to get along most roads, even if progress is sometimes slow.

Riding a bike is great for building up stamina. Take it easy at first if you are inexperienced, and don't attempt to cover more than a few miles in one go. Pretty soon you will find you are able to clock up more and more miles. It's fun to fix a computer to your bike so that you can see how fast and far you are going.

The Seven Sisters – an unspoilt stretch of coastal scenery.

You seldom see a cyclist who is fat or smoking a cigarette. Most look much fitter than the average motorist, and that's because nearly all of them are. Riding bikes, as you might expect, is particularly good for building up strength in the legs, but you'll be surprised how good it is for stomach and arm muscles, too.

All that fresh air won't do you any harm at all, especially if you can manage to avoid the fumes belched out by some inconsiderate drivers. And it won't matter if you get wet, unless you are soaked to the skin and can't find anywhere to dry off afterwards.

Riding bikes doesn't cause pressure on joints in the same way as running, but the exercise is equally beneficial. And why bother to ride an exercise bike in a gym when you can get outside and ride the real thing in the open air?

Efficiency

Many bikes are to be found sitting in sheds, garages or even lofts, gathering dust for a variety of reasons. It may be that people find them too much like hard work or that they don't like riding them in the wet, but chiefly I think it's because they don't feel safe or comfortable on them.

We have become so motorised as a nation that, for many people, cars seem to be the only way to travel. But when you have thousands of cars in the most crowded part of one of the most crowded countries in the world, their advantages of speed and enjoyment are quickly lost.

Bikes, on the other hand, are the most efficient form of human-powered transport known to man (or to woman or child). They are cheap to buy and have almost no running costs. They keep you fit and they are fun.

Yes, they can be hard work up hills, against the wind and in the rain, but nobody will force you to meet any of those challenges – and when you do, you'll find that they can be surprisingly invigorating. On the flat, with the wind behind you, cycling is supremely enjoyable, and going down a hill is absolute bliss.

Bikes are remarkably quick in towns: the annual commuter challenge race between Hove and Brighton is invariably won by a cyclist. They also go at just the right speed for you to be able to see things around you without getting bored.

In a car you are concentrating on road safety. On foot, progress can be too slow to be interesting, unless you are in superb countryside. But cycling along at about ten miles an hour is ideal.

Yes, bikes can be dangerous if you ride poorly on busy main roads, but if you are sensible and take the back doubles there is little risk – and, as we shall see, safe new cycleways are being built all the time.

A good way to get started is to join a guided cycle ride, such as one of those in East Sussex County Council's popular Cyling East Sussex programme. Many of the rides are aimed at beginners, and you will benefit from both the experience of the leader and the sociability of the group you ride with.

This book, like those guided rides, is designed not only for families looking for safe and attractive routes, but for the novice or nervous cyclist who wants to take to two wheels but needs a little encouragement. It unashamedly peddles pedalling as the very best way to see Sussex.

"There is no need for a perfectly reasonable bike for the average rider to cost more than about £300, and some are far cheaper than that. A bike is a bargain"

Buying a bike

Since a bike can last a lifetime, it's worth choosing one carefully. Unlike cars, they depreciate slowly, and with careful maintenance they remain in excellent order for years.

Many big retailers offer them, and they can be bought by mail order often at ridiculously low prices: I have even seen them for sale in supermarkets. It is best, however, to go to a specialist bike shop of the kind that is available in almost every town of more than 10,000 people, and sometimes even in villages. They may not always be the cheapest, although most are pretty competitive these days, but they can offer advice and experience that is extremely valuable to riders in the long run. Many of them also offer maintenance deals.

What kind of bike do you want? Is it simply for pootling about town on flat roads, or are you going to use it mainly for riding over the Downs? Make a note of your needs before you go to the shop, and don't rule out the possibility of having more than one for different conditions if your cash will stretch that far.

There are many different types of bikes. Here's a brief guide:

Town bikes

Traditionally these were the heavy sit-up-and beg models much favoured by policemen and old ladies. Although they are still made by a few specialist firms, most people prefer something equally durable but a little more sporty. All major firms produce a good range of these bikes and they will suit a great many people who want a reliable, safe steed. These days they come with anything from five to 21 gears, all simple to operate, so it's easy to get up hills on them.

Sports bikes

These are usually more expensive than town bikes, and are really for people who like going fairly fast along country roads. They are nippy and light, but not suitable for going over rough tracks. Most have drop handlebars, which the average rider will find uncomfortable.

Racing bikes

These are the ultra-light
models, often extremely
expensive, that you see
ridden at speed by keenists in
groups on Sunday mornings,
often pedalling in formation
and wearing Lycra shorts.
They are remarkably fast and
responsive but are strictly for
speed merchants. If you really
want one you're probably
reading the wrong book!

Mountain bikes

There is no doubting the
enormous effect that these
bikes have had on the
industry. They have helped
turn cycling from something
rather 'nerdy' into what is

First man home: Chris Gordon-Coker
needed a racing bike to complete the
2000 London to Brighton Bike Ride in
2hours 43 minutes – but most of us
will be looking for something a little
more sedate.

now regarded as an admirably cool and athletic hobby.

Mountain bikes vary enormously in price. I have seen
them advertised for less than £50, while at the other end of
the scale you can pay several thousand pounds for them. A
good dealer will advise you, but the average rider should be
able to buy a perfectly acceptable bike for £200–£300.

Choose your model according to how sporting you are. If
you intend to travel mainly on the road, forget it, because
the thick tyres tend to drag, but for riding off-road (*see page 41*)
they are ideal.

All of them have plenty of gears, and the gears are much
easier to cope with than in days gone by. Some bikes also
have suspension, which is useful if you are riding a lot over
bumpy paths.

Many of them don't have mudguards, so remember that
you may get a wet bottom on damp days or when speeding
through puddles.

Hybrids

As the name suggests, these are a cross between a mountain bike and a roadster. They can be a good compromise for many riders, and the best of them are superb. Prices range from a couple of hundred pounds to far more than that.

Small wheeled bikes

Moultons and their successors caused a big sensation in the 1960s and for a time threatened to dominate the market, but their limitations soon became clear. Generally they are harder than conventional bikes to push over the same distance. Their huge advantage is their flexibility and their portability. They take up less space at home and can often be taken in cars.

Folding bikes

The best of the folding bikes, such as the Brompton, are marvellous pieces of machinery, expertly designed. They have the same defects and virtues as small-wheeled bikes, which they invariably are, but with the extra advantage of even more portability. Some of them fold so small that they can even be taken as luggage on planes and in trains.

Beware, though, of cheap models in this range. They are often not worth buying, because they are much more prone to mechanical failure and, being made of cheap materials, they are often harder to ride.

Do make sure, if you buy one, that you can work the folding mechanism, or the bike will be more trouble than it is worth.

Ladies' bikes

Some women feel insecure with the crossbar fitted to conventional cycles. Traditional ladies' bikes do without them and can still be fairly sporty. On mountain bikes, which tend to have small frames, women often find the crossbar less of a problem. Many women's bikes also have broader and more comfortable saddles adjusted to their shape.

Children's bikes

These range from tiny bikes with stabilisers for very young children just learning to ride to models which are close to adult size. It's seldom worth spending huge sums on them unless you have a large family, because kids grow quickly and the average bike will last them only about five years. The bikes can often make useful presents to friends if kept in good order.

Second hand bikes

Some reputable dealers will come up with real bargains. Otherwise, be careful: if you buy one from a shop window or a newspaper ad, you have only your own eyes and common sense to work out whether it's a bargain, whether it will suit you and, above all, whether it is safe.

Tandems

Bicycles made for two have been current since Victorian times. They are faster than ordinary bikes along the flat and down hills, but hard work up them. Tandems are great when you have two riders of unequal strength and stamina, for the strong one can help the weaker rider.

They are cumbersome, not at all portable, and rather expensive, You have to make sure you buy one that suits the needs of both parties. Remember that on the back you have no control over the steering. They can be great fun, and I have ridden one regularly with sundry partners since 1965.

Trailer bikes

These are the one-wheeled contraptions fastened to the back of conventional bikes that you often see children riding on behind adults. They have the same advantages as tandems but are more portable and flexible. They are easy to fix on and are highly recommended.

Trailers

It's surprising what you can carry on a bike, and a trailer adds to the capacity. They are mightily useful for camping but are hard work up hills. Some trailers have been adapted to carry children safely and comfortably.

Whatever kind of bike you ride, make sure that it's the right size. Many people buy cycles which are too small for them, and they suffer as a result. When sitting on the saddle, the leg should be fairly fully extended when the pedal is far away from you, and you should be able to touch the ground with the ball of your foot. The handlebars should generally be about the same height as the saddle.

There is no need for a perfectly reasonable bike for the average rider to cost more than about £300, and some are far cheaper than that. A bike is a bargain.

Fully kitted out: a young family outside Sackville College, East Grinstead.

Accessories

Once you have bought a bike, you will almost certainly need some accessories. The most important of these is a pump. Make sure that it fits the valves of your bike. There are three types: Woods, Presta and Schrader valves. Your cycle dealer will tell you which kind you need.

Lights

Lights will be needed if you intend to travel by night. Once heavy and cumbersome, they are now extremely convenient and weigh very little. It's best to take them off when not in use, because they are attractive to thieves. The alternative is a dynamo, which requires some effort to push and will not shine when you stop. The advantages are that it is almost theft-proof and doesn't need batteries.

By law you must also have a red rear reflector when riding a bike at night. A spacer (a horizontal rod with a reflector attached), is good for encouraging cars to give you a wide berth. Reflectors fitted on wheels ensure people can see you from the side.

Security

Locks are essential because bikes are stolen so often. Always make sure that you lock a bike to an object – preferably a bike stand but, if not, to railings or even a small tree. The best kind is a D lock, available from any dealer. It is rather heavy, but difficult even for determined thieves to break. If you have detachable wheels, make sure that they are locked up, too. Expensive saddles are best taken with you when you stop. The cheaper the bike, the less likely it is to be stolen, although I have had eight pinched so far and none of them was a piece of rocket science.

Child seats

Children up to about five years old can be carried on child seats. There are good models available, mainly made of plastic although some are of metal. Make sure that the seat is fitted properly and that it has a harness in case the child falls asleep. Most children enjoy being carried on bikes, but remember that it can be cold for them in winter, and that the view of your back is a bit restricting.

Luggage

You will want something to carry around your belongings, whether they be coats, tools, picnics or maps. I have already mentioned trailers, but they are suitable only for large loads.

Baskets, usually fixed to the front, are good for light shopping, but things can fall through the holes or bounce out. Many bikes have carriers fitted to the back, and these are good for supporting bags, which can be secured by using elastic straps. The carriers are also essential if you have panniers. These are good for carrying fairly heavy loads, as the weight is carried low down on the bike, but they can be a nuisance to lug about once you have stopped.

 Saddlebags are usually weatherproof and fit easily on to the back of a bike. Some riders have handlebar bags, good for small items such as cameras, and you can also get small bags and pouches which slip under the saddle and on to the bike frame, but attaching a carrier to your person is in many ways the best option. A rucksack is very useful once you have dismounted, but it has rather a high centre of gravity and can be sweaty in wet weather. Many cyclists prefer to wear a 'bum bag', which has neither of these disadvantages and which is a particularly good way of carrying luggage off-road, where strapping the load to your body rather than the bike offers the best suspension.

Helmets

Should you wear a helmet or not? Most bike books will say you should. I confess that I have never worn one in my life, preferring the freedom that a bike gives. Helmets are compulsory on motor bikes because these machines travel fast and you are likely to hurt your head if you fall off, but on a bike you are not generally in much danger of that because of slower speeds.

The danger is caused by other vehicles on the road hitting you, so there is a greater case for helmets on busy roads and less of one elsewhere unless you are planning high speed descents on a mountain bike. For children, though, the case for helmets is much stronger on any surface.

Good cycle dealers will give you advice about helmets. If you use one, it must be well fitted, fastened securely and properly ventilated.

Clothing

Make sure you wear clothes that are loose and not too bulky. Shorts are comfortable on all but the coldest days. Cycling makes you hot, so don't wear too much.

If you wear trousers, either tuck them into your socks or use cycle clips to prevent them getting caught in the chain. Mittens or gloves are essential in cold weather as hands can get cold. Warm, preferably waterproof, shoes are needed on winter days, but I find sports sandals comfortable in the summer. Special cycling shoes can be bought if you like to fit toe clips on the pedals. Many inexperienced riders find these clips awkward.

In wet weather, make sure that you wear something which is waterproof but made of fabric that breathes. Capes were once popular, but they can get caught in the wind and it is sometimes hard to make signals in them.

Spares

I always carry a pump with me and a small bag of spares. These include a puncture repair outfit, tyre levers, a spanner, a screwdriver, an Allen key and a spare light bulb. If you are going on long journeys more equipment is necessary, such as brake cables, brake blocks and a spare inner tube. I always tuck a rag or J-cloth under the saddle to clean my hands or the bike.

Maintenance

M odern bikes are not like the ones many people remember from long ago. They have up to 21 gears rather than three, and they all click into place firmly. The bikes are generally much more reliable.

But things can still go wrong with them. By far the most common problem is a puncture. It is best to take out a pump and a repair kit with you so that repairs can be carried out on the spot. (*See next page.*) It takes a bit of practice to get it right, but follow the instructions carefully and you should be all right. Punctures are the one repair that most dealers will not do for you, because it simply isn't worth their while.

Other simple maintenance is worth carrying out regularly to make bikes last longer. Always wipe them down when they have been out in the rain or through mud. Clean and oil bikes either every 100 miles or every week, depending on how much use you give them. Oil all moving parts, but don't put on too much.

Keep the tyres well pumped up, using a hand pump rather than a mechanical one so that you don't overdo it. Regularly check that no bolts are coming loose and that the brakes are working.

What you do beyond that depends upon your level of expertise. Some people pride themselves on carrying out their own repairs. Most, like me, prefer to have anything more complicated carried out by a skilled mechanic.

I also put my bike in for a service every six months. The cost is reasonable, and the mechanic is able to pick up any faults I may have missed. The bike always runs sweetly afterwards. Many firms offer free services in the early months of a new bike's life.

Even if you pay for regular maintenance, the cost of running a bike is often not much more than a penny a mile – cheap in comparison with any form of motorised transport. It's yet another advantage of cycling.

How to mend a puncture

Here is a simple step-by-step guide to mending a puncture:

1. Turn the bike upside down and undo the lock nut on the valve so that it can be removed.

2. Deflate the tube if any air is left in it, and use tyre levers to take off one side of the outer tyre, being careful not to pinch the innertube.

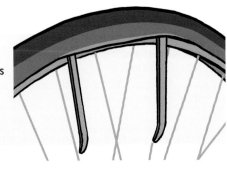

3. Remove the innertube – there is no need to take the wheel off – and pump it up until you can hear where the air is coming from. If this doesn't work, put the tube in a bucket of water and locate the puncture from the bubbles.

4. Thoroughly clean and dry the innertube in the area of the puncture. Open the puncture outfit case and, using the rasp or sandpaper provided, roughen up the tube so that the patch will stick. Using yellow crayon, mark a cross on the exact area of the puncture.

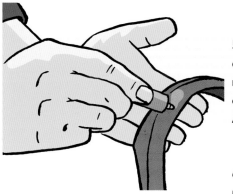

5. Deflate the tube completely, and squeeze a modest amount of adhesive on to the innertube. Allow it to dry thoroughly.

6. Peel off a suitably sized patch from the strip provided, taking off the foil and paper covering. Press it firmly on to the adhesive, pushing down strongly, especially at the edges. Lightly dust with French chalk to prevent it sticking to the outer tyre.

7. Examine the outer tyre to see if you can find the cause of the puncture – perhaps a thorn, a stone or a piece of glass – and remove it.

8. Slightly inflate the innertube and then carefully push it back under the outer tyre, with the valve in its correct position, taking great care not to pinch the tube. Replace the valve nut.

9. Replace the outer tyre, using your fingers if possible. If you use the tyre levers, again exercise great care not to damage the inner-tube.

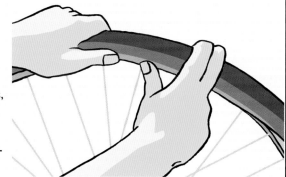

10. Pump up the tyre as hard as possible – and with luck you will be merrily on your way!

Safety

Oone of the biggest worries for the novice rider, or indeed for someone who has not ridden a bike for some time, is safety. Cycling can look awfully precarious to a motorist, and some riders seem intent on a daily dice with death.

Use your common sense, however, and you will be as safe as any other road user. You will certainly be less at risk than motor cyclists, because they are travelling at speed on powerful machines.

Your bike in itself is unlikely to injure you. Most riders do not exceed 15mph on the flat, and many go at much slower speeds. Even if you fall off, the chances are that you will not hurt yourself much, if at all.

The danger is posed by other road users. Cars, especially, can be lethal, particularly when driven at more than 30mph. It has to be said that most car drivers are very considerate to cyclists, giving them a wide berth, but a stubborn minority are not. Indeed there are some drivers to whom a bike appears to be invisible.

There are a few tips that are worth taking. Always keep well over to your side of the road, but leave about three feet from the pavement. This means that you do not have to ride in the gutter and have a little room for avoiding action if someone comes past too close for comfort.

Keep a steady course wherever possible. Don't ride like a maniac, but don't ride too slowly either, or you will be a nuisance to other road users by wobbling about.

Always make your intentions clear by giving good hand signals well in advance of the manoeuvre you are about to make. Look behind you to make sure there is nothing on your tail, especially when turning right. If you are nervous, or if there is a long stream of traffic, get off your bike by the kerb and wheel it across the junction.

Make sure that you have a bell or hooter on the bike, and use it when people loom into view. You have to make other road users, especially motorists, aware of your presence. At junctions, fix them with your eye so they know you are there.

Obey the Highway Code. Don't go through red lights, as so many cyclists do these days, and don't ride on pavements.

Safety last!

Ensure you are seen at night by fixing lights and reflectors on your bike. Wear reflective clothing or bands if possible – it's amazing how effective this is.

Remember that you can travel pretty fast down hills, and that you therefore need to react accordingly. The trick is knowing how quickly you can stop in an emergency: it may require a greater distance than you think. In wet weather roads can become slippery and skiddy. Be particularly careful where you see patches of oil and grease in the road. Stopping distances are much greater in the wet than in the dry, and you must adjust to that.

This applies even more in snow or ice. It's amazing how easy it is to ride a two-wheeler in these conditions, but be careful. Thick snow is sometimes quite hard to ride in, but the grip is good. Black ice is the most dangerous of all, especially down hills. Try not to put your brakes on at all when riding on ice: if you have to, apply them gradually.

In fog, make sure even more than usual that you can be seen, and of course put your lights on. If necessary, walk on the pavement.

Riding bikes in thunderstorms is pretty safe in towns but not advisable on high, lonely roads in the country. Find shelter if you can, but not under single trees.

Make full use of a bike's flexibility in slipping through the traffic, but beware at all times of the driver who hasn't seen you or the passenger who is about to open a door in your face. Above all, be aware of the conditions and the traffic.

You are allowed to ride two abreast except on busy narrow roads, but it's best to ride singly where two cars are passing each other. Simply use your common sense.

Many people, understandably, are particularly worried about children. I was brought up in London and rode from the age of six along busy streets in the centre of the town without mishap. Few, if any, parents would allow their children to do that today. Nonetheless, they can learn to ride bikes as soon as they can balance – and the earlier the better.

Once their stablisers are taken off, the fun starts in teaching them to keep upright. Some small bikes these days come with a long stick which can be slotted under the saddle to prevent the hapless adult getting severe backache while hanging on to the bike.

Young children are allowed to ride on the pavement, and this is the best place for them. After that you can progress to a cycle track or a quiet country lane. Make sure that they have developed a good road sense before you allow them anywhere near traffic.They vary enormously in this, as well as in their general riding ability, but I have found that by nine or ten they are usually safe for the road if accompanied.

The adult should ride on the outside when riding two-abreast. If conditions are at all dangerous, move over to the pavement or to the side of the road and walk until it is safe again. Children are even less visible to the average motorist than adults, so make them conspicuous: bright clothing is useful, and reflecting bands or jackets help, too.

You can buy spacers from good cycle dealers. Fitted to the sides of bikes, they make motorists give you a wider than usual berth. Some parents also like to fix tall flags to the back of small bikes to make them noticeable. These are handy to fix to trailer bikes, trailers and sidecars, and it's surprising how effective they are.

It's a pity that modern road conditions make all this necessary, but most children enjoy cycling, and on quiet roads or special cycle paths the risks of accident and injury are small.

Remember that the more people ride bikes, the more drivers will pay attention and the more councils will provide cycle tracks. It's a virtuous circle, as round and satisfying as the spin of a bicycle wheel.

Hiring bikes

You may not have a bike of your own. You may not want to invest in a new machine until you have tried one out. You may be somewhere far away from home and fancy a ride.

Hiring a bike is often worthwhile, but you will find that the cost varies enormously. One of the first bikes I ever hired (in 1965) cost just half a crown a week – good value even then. You are likely to be set back £50 or more for something even half-decent these days.

If you are into serious cycling, go to a reputable dealer. It really doesn't matter half as much if you are just messing around on flat cycle paths for an hour or two.

Ensure that the bike is the right height for you and that you feel comfortable on it. Check the gears to make sure they all work, and thump the tyres to ensure that they are pumped up properly. Look the thing over to make sure that there are no glaring faults: apart from anything else, you might be blamed for them afterwards.

Remember that most bike hire firms ask for a deposit as well as the hire charge. They should also lend you a lock to keep the bike secure should you choose to park it anywhere,

Bike hire firms usually choose suitable locations, such as at the West Pier in Brighton by the cycle lane, or at Exceat close to Friston Forest. They are also often located next to railway stations.

All kinds of bikes can be hired, ranging from mountain bikes (always the most popular) to roadsters. Tandems and trailer bikes are also often available.

Although you should always be careful when first riding a bike which is new to you, it's surprising how quickly you can get used to machines which seem exceedingly strange for the first few pushes.

"When cyclists moan about the lack of purpose-built tracks and paths in Sussex I sometimes remind them that 30 years ago there were none at all"

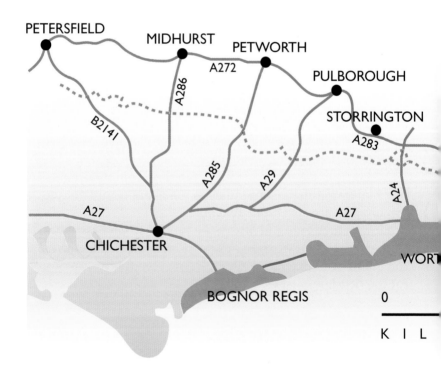

Cycle paths in the country

*T*he first cycle path I can recall being built in Sussex, a
modest effort linking the county town of Lewes to the
little village of Kingston only a mile and half away, ought to
have a plaque at each end recording that this was a
pioneering venture. It was quickly followed by a much more
important trail, however, and now we have a cornucopia of
cycle tracks compared with the dreary days of yesteryear –
and there are many more to come.

The South Downs Way

This magnificent long-distance path (*see map below, and a
section of the route on page 60*) runs from Winchester to
Eastbourne, but for the purposes of a book called *Cycling
Sussex* starts at the Hampshire border. It is unusual among
Britain's paths in being a bridleway, which means that
cyclists (and horse riders) as well as walkers can, and do,

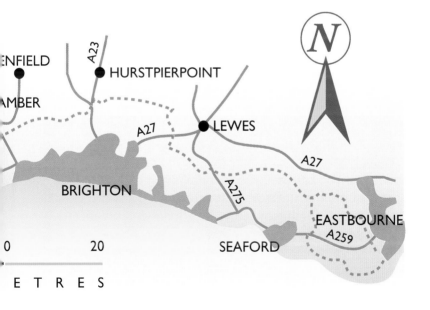

use it. Note that between Alfriston and Eastbourne the route offers two separate options: a coastal footpath for walkers only and an inland bridleway which cyclists may use.

There's no doubt that this is the king of the cycle tracks in Sussex. For most of its 80 miles it goes along the ridge of the Downs, offering superb views on fine days.

Jack and Jill: the windmills are a famous sight on the Sussex Downs above Clayton.

Over the past 30 years most of the difficult crossings of main roads and the awkward sections along them have been ironed out. The biggest boost of all was a bridge over the River Adur near Upper Beeding, and the second best was another bridge built more recently over the River Arun north of Houghton.

Although some rides later in the book traverse short stretches of it, this route really is not for novice cyclists. It is extremely steep in many places, and the terrain can be awkward. You can feel extremely exposed up on the Downs during sudden squalls or great gales, and the South Downs Way is really suitable over any length only for riders on mountain bikes.

Riding on it is an incomparable experience, however, and it's worth getting reasonably fit or proficient just to enjoy being up there on a bike.

The Downs Link

This track links the South Downs near Upper Beeding with the North Downs close to Guildford. Most of the 30-mile route is on old railway tracks which once ran from Shoreham to Horsham and from Horsham to Guildford before Dr Beeching's notorious cuts.

For most of its length it runs in Sussex, going through Bramber, Henfield and Partridge Green, before reaching Christ's Hospital and bypassing Horsham to head north out of the county.

The views are not outstanding, because the tracks often pass through cuttings, and there are one or two awkward diversions – especially north of Beeding, where the route takes a path through a field. The terrain can be very wet here after heavy rain.

But the Downs Link is fairly flat, well marked and often extremely sylvan. It's a good starter route for riding off-road, and a fine alternative to many busy north-south roads in West Sussex.

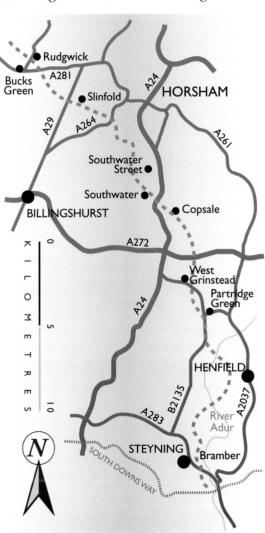

The Coastal Link

It may be short – only just over two miles from the old toll bridge at Shoreham to the junction of the South Downs Way and the Downs Link, close to the former Beeding cement works – but this is one of the most popular and useful cycle tracks in Sussex. It runs close to the A27 and the A259, and we follow it on p. 64. There is easy parking nearby, and it is less than a mile from the railway station at Shoreham.

This is a well-paved and well-maintained path along an old railway line and by the River Adur, with some amusing sculptures by the side. The Link is ideal for a novice rider trying out a track for the first time, but its real value is in connecting the urban area with two great countryside trails.

The Worth Way

This is a seven-mile cycleway linking Three Bridges near Crawley with the historic town of East Grinstead. Nearly all of it is along an old railway track, and it is extremely well marked. Although it passes through a heavily populated part of North Sussex, it feels quite rural for most of its length. The whole of the Way is incorporated into one of the rides later on in this book (*see page 76*).

The terrain is good and there are hardly any hills. There are existing railway stations at either end. This really is ideal for a short ride, and there are many attractions only a mile or two off the route.

The Forest Way

Here is another old railway track which has been converted into a path which cyclists can use. Starting just outside East Grinstead, it carries on almost to Groombridge on the Kent border. A ride based on it can be found later in this book (*see page 56*).

This area is less built up than land surrounding the Worth Way, and the route can feel quite remote in places, but in truth you are never far from civilisation. Once again, because it is flat and well surfaced, it is an ideal route for beginners. It is nine and a half miles long.

The Cuckoo Trail

This 11-mile long path is the flagship for cycle routes in East Sussex – the result of a joint project between Wealden District Council, East Sussex County Council and Sustrans, the cycle track building charity.

Running from Polegate to Heathfield, it follows the line of the old branch railway which once continued to Eridge. The trail was opened in 1994.

The best-used section, between Polegate and Hailsham, has a metalled surface. The rest of the trail, through Hellingly and Horam to Heathfield, is well surfaced and marked with excellent sculptures by the side.

Only three short stretches are on the road, and safe crossings have been provided over a few busy roads which cross its path. It is a deservedly popular trail which cyclists of all ages and ability can enjoy.

Routes are being devised south of the trail to Eastbourne, to the Seven Sisters and to Newhaven.

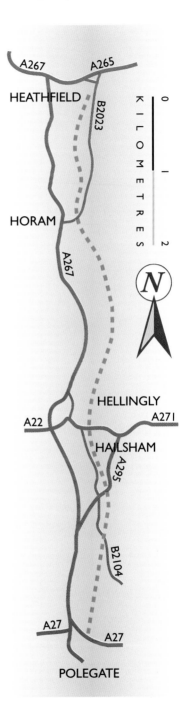

The Ouse is tidal as far north as Barcombe Mills, a tranquil spot where the river flows alongside several fast-flowing cuts.

The Dyke Railway

A cycle track leads from the Downsman pub in Hangleton Way on the edge of the built up area of Hove, following the track of the old Dyke Railway along to Brighton and Hove Golf Club – where it deviates from the old line before joining the Devil's Dyke Road. This is one of the oldest cycle tracks in Sussex and a handy way of leaving Brighton and Hove to reach the Downs. Not far away is the Benfield Valley cycle path, which goes from close to the junction of Hangleton Road and Old Shoreham Road past the Sainsbury's super-store to Hangleton Lane. Although not much more than a mile long, it is another good route out of the town and is surprisingly pleasant to ride on. Both these routes are used in a short ride later in the book (*see page 44*).

The Centurion Way

This is another excellent project from Sustrans, built on a former section of the Chichester to Midhurst railway, and it starts right in the car park of Chichester Station. (*See page 80 for a ride following this route.*)

Using quiet paths and roads, it then heads into open country while still skirting the city. It lands up at East Lavant, which is the gateway to all kinds of glorious countryside on the Downs around Goodwood.

A link has already been provided westwards to Bosham, and it is now planned to take the path northwards to West Dean. Eventually it will link up with the South Downs Way.

Barcombe Mills

This bridleway may be only a mile long, but it is extremely useful. It connects Barcombe Mills, with its tea room and attractive water features (*see photograph left*), with the Anchor pub further up the River Ouse, where boats can be hired and beer supped.

Bike routes in town

*T*he cycle tracks in the previous section are so enjoyable because they are mainly in the country and off the road. They don't, however, always provide the quickest way of getting about – and in any case, most people in Sussex live in towns.

These days, thankfully, there is an imperfect but growing network of cycle routes both between many of the main towns and within them. (*See page 101 for enquiring about new routes.*) It is well worth getting to know where they are, since for nervous riders they can make all the difference between going out with confidence and not riding a bike at all.

Brighton and Hove

The biggest conurbation in the county, with more than 250,000 people, also has one of the best cycle routes – all the way along the front from Hove Lagoon to the Palace Pier, a distance of around three miles. It was a struggle for cycling organisations to get it constructed, and it could do with improvement, but it is still probably the best-used cycle route of all.

For most of the way it goes along the south pavement of Kingsway and King's Road, the main A259 coast route. As this thoroughfare is used by 30,000 motorised vehicles daily, it's as well to escape from it and take the cycle path if you can. Parts of the surface are far too bumpy (especially in Brighton), the corners are too sharp and there is some curious routing, but overall it is a huge bonus for bikes. In time, it will be extended eastwards towards Rottingdean and west through Shoreham Harbour towards Worthing.

There is also a cycle route from Grand Parade northwards towards The Level, and it's a pity that no provision has been made to connect it over 300 yards or so to the seafront track. However, cyclists can always walk this distance if they choose. The route largely uses pavements in the central garden area, and has its own crossings over busy roads. Another gap exists along the Lewes Road shopping area of

Brighton's cycle lane near the Old Steine.

the A270, although this is to be rectified soon by Brighton and Hove Council. But north of the busy Vogue Gyratory junction there is now a cycleway all the way to Lewes. This goes within Brighton itself on each side of the main road, but north of Coldean Lane there is a separate cycle path on the left hand side of the road. It passes the two universities and Falmer village before descending towards Newmarket and Lewes.

It can be rather a slog, and the wind always seems to be against you, but riding along this path is infinitely preferable to the alternative – sharing the main road with juggernauts going at least 70mph.

There are advisory cycle routes through the North Laine area of Brighton followed by another cycle route along the A23 by Preston Park. Eventually this will be continued all the way up to Patcham, which will be excellent news for riders who currently have to share the road with thousands of vehicles on their way to and from a busy coastal resort.

More short stretches of cycleway have been provided at other town centre locations, and at many junctions cyclists have a stop line in advance of other traffic. Bikes can also go along parts of North Street and Western Road where all other traffic except buses and taxis are banned.

In Dyke Road and Dyke Road Avenue, which lead from Seven Dials out of Brighton and Hove towards the Devil's Dyke, there is a cycle lane in the road but cars are allowed to park in it. Although it is better than nothing, in that at least drivers are made aware of the presence of cyclists, it is a distinctly curious arrangement.

North of Brighton there is one of the longest cycleways in the county heading all the way to Crawley. This was put in when the A23 was widened but was obviously not designed by a cyclist. Riders have to take an amazingly convoluted and hilly route, particularly at Pyecombe, while the start and finish close to the Brighton bypass leave a lot to be desired.

Much of the cycleway is on a track close to the A23, which means that riders are barely separated from the busiest road in Sussex. It is hardly a pleasure using these stretches, but once again is much safer than it used to be when riders had no alternative other than to use the road. There are other bits which use old stretches of the A23, such as the section through Sayers Common. Although these are shared with some local traffic, they are much more pleasant because they are away from the main roar of the traffic.

There are ambitious plans for improving cycleways within Brighton and Hove, including connecting the Dyke Railway route through Hove towards the seafront, but the cycling budget is tiny and it may be many years before a proper cycling network has been completed.

Adur

The most notable feature for cyclists in Adur is the Coastal Link connecting Shoreham to the Downs (*see pages 30 and 64*). Otherwise there isn't much, but the South Coast Cycleway will make all the difference when it has been built.

Arun

This is such a rural district that there is little need for many dedicated cycle routes, but there is a good cycleway for most of the length of the busy main road from Chichester to Bognor. The council has also produced three excellent leaflets covering off-road routes on the Downs – one around Slindon and Bignor, one around the Arun Valley and the third connecting Cissbury and Chanctonbury Rings. There are also cycleways along the A27, on the way to Worthing, and riders can use some of the old sections of the road which were left when new dual carriageway sections were built, such as at Clapham.

Chichester

The excellent Centurion Way (*see page 33*) comes right into the town and the cycleway to Bognor starts at the bypass roundabout.

There is a cycle track on the road which passes the Chichester Festival Theatre leading north to Lavant. Bikes can use the towpath of the canal (*below*), and there are short lengths of cycleways next to the bypass. There is a link to Fishbourne where the Roman palace is.

Through traffic is discouraged from the city centre, which means that biking can be a pleasure, especially as the terrain is flat. The district council has produced an excellent map of advisory cycle routes. These also include quiet routes leading out of the city to places such as North Mundham, Oving, Westhampnett, Lavant and Apuldram.

Further out, there are well marked links to the delightful harbour village of Bosham and to Tangmere.

A view along the Chichester Canal.

Crawley

An excellent network of cycle routes is slowly being built up in this new town, where the road network is more conducive to cycling than in many older towns.

Once this has been completed, it will be possible to travel by bike through the greater part of Crawley in safety. There are already good links along much of the old A23 and from Three Bridges Station to the Worth Way, and you can cycle directly from Crawley to Brighton. The council is developing routes into most of the neighbourhoods surrounding the town centre, the prime example being the network which extends to the new Maidenbower area.

Existing routes already include those along Fleming Way, Manor Royal, Southgate Avenue and into Furnace Green. There is even a link right into Gatwick Airport which, although not used by many passengers, is useful to some of the people who work there.

Eastbourne

Here is another town making a valiant effort on behalf of cyclists. There are lengths of cycleway around the general hospital and down Lottbridge Drove. The Cuckoo Trail (*see page 31*) is being connected to the town centre in an exciting development, and the new Sovereign Harbour scheme is being linked to the main seafront. When all this has been completed, there will be eight miles of routes in the town, with an extension linking the harbour to local caravan parks and Pevensey Bay. In Eastbourne town centre, and at other locations, too, plenty of GRIPPA lockable cycle stands have been installed.

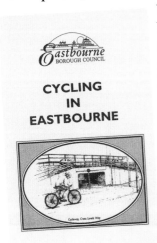

Eastbourne is one of several towns which produce guides for cyclists.

Hastings

The main development in this fine old coastal town is the seafront cycle lane, which is similar in concept to that in Brighton but better because it was planned later. It runs from Grosvenor Gardens in St Leonards past Marine and Eversfield Place to Robertson Street all along the promenade. A safe crossing of the A259 linking the promenade track with the town centre is being built, and an extension along the back of the beach to link up with the existing cyce track at Glyne Gap, Bexhill, is another development very much on the cards.

The two county councils are passionate advocates of cycling and other 'green' pursuits.

Horsham

The Downs Link (*see page 29*) passes through many miles of the district and there are other lanes allowing riders to avoid busy roads such as the A272 and the A24. The council has also produced a well-mapped series of ten cycle routes which show off this lovely part of the countryside to best advantage.

Lewes

The town itself may be very hilly, but there is a cycleway part way to Kingston which is well worth using, and another from Cliffe High Street along the river heading north which is highly attractive. A useful cycle link has been built along the A27 east of Southerham to connect with Ranscombe Lane and Glynde. Plenty of small lanes enable cyclists to avoid the main roads.

Mid Sussex

A cycle lane has been constructed between Hassocks and Burgess Hill, enabling riders to avoid the busy main road. A host of small lanes parallel to the A23 enables the discerning cyclist to avoid that route, although there is also a cycleway alongside or close to it.

Rother

Routes are at an embryo stage in this district, but the council says it is very excited about getting them up and running. Some of the most popular routes are in the extreme east of the area, notably a highly successful link between Rye and Camber which is used daily by a large number of school-children.

Wealden

The district council deserves top marks for getting on so well with the Cuckoo Trail (*see page 31*). The Forest Way (*see page 30*) is a good traffic-free route which connects Groombridge and East Grinstead. As in many parts of rural Sussex, there is a magnificent network of minor roads which can be used instead of difficult main routes such as the A22.

Worthing

There is a cycle route along the prom but it has proved surprisingly controversial because of a few well-publicised accidents. The seafront is relatively traffic-free apart from right by the pier, so it is possible to cycle along it reasonably safely. Further links are being prepared in some of the outskirts, notably around Ferring.

Off-road cycling

*T*here are few better feelings than standing by your bike on the top of a hill somewhere in the countryside with stunning views of Sussex all around you. It's even better when you are on a track where there is no traffic at all.

This can easily be achieved through off-road cycling, which has grown enormously in popularity over the last twenty years. I can remember when almost no one ventured on to tracks and paths, whereas now it is common practice.

The main reason is the introduction of the mountain bike, one of the most significant developments in cycling over the last century. The robust construction of these bikes makes it easy for riders to go over rough terrain. They have thick, wide tyres and good suspension.

It is, of course, possible to ride other forms of bike off road, notably hybrids, but tandems are not a lot of fun because of their long wheelbase and racing bikes are far too skimpy. Mountain bikes are designed for this kind of riding, although the irony is that most people who own them never take them into the countryside at all.

Off-road cycling varies greatly. You can potter gently along some of the cycleways I have described in other parts of this book, such as the Cuckoo Trail and the Worth Way – former railway lines which are flat and in many cases well surfaced. On the Downs and in other hilly parts of the county, on the other hand, there are tracks with rough surfaces and steep slopes where skill is needed to stay upright.

Loose gravel and stones will always make riding more difficult, and you should be particularly careful when going downhill on this kind of surface. Remember also that rain always makes surfaces more slippery, and that mud is mighty hard to cycle through. On winter days you may also have to be careful of snow and ice, but overcoming tough conditions can be part of the joy of off-road cycling.

Mountain bikes always come with gears. The simplest

ones have only five, but most have 21 these days, and some
have even more. The low gears enable you to ride up hills in
a way that old-fashioned gears on roadster bikes never
could, and they enable riders of average fitness to negotiate
longish inclines. Hills can be regarded as challenges, but you
should never be ashamed to get off and walk where they are
particularly tough or hazardous. There are also steep slopes
where sometimes it's advisable to get off even when going
downhill.

We are extremely fortunate in Sussex with the amount of
off-road tracks available to us. The most exhilarating route
of all is the South Downs Way, which I describe elsewhere
(*see page 27*), but there are several other well-marked and
defined tracks.

You can also cycle on any bridleway (marked with a blue
arrow on signs), or on roads used as a public path. There are
hundreds of miles of these all over the county, and they are
easily identifiable on Ordnance Survey maps. You can
create your own circular journeys using these tracks: there's
a lot of pleasure to be derived from riding routes you have
worked out for yourself.

Do always give way to pedestrians and horses. You may
find a lot of these on well-used routes such as the South
Downs Way but the glory of most bridleways is that even in
a crowded county such as Sussex, they tend to be empty.

Please don't ride on footpaths. They may well look
tempting, but cycling is not allowed on them, usually for
very good reasons. They tend to be narrower than bridleways and often have obstacles such as stiles. If you find it
necessary to use one, walk the bike along it instead.

You will never be far from civilisation in Sussex, but make
sure when you set out that you have suitable clothing with
you, because the weather always seems more extreme when
you are out in the countryside, especially on high ground.
Take some refreshment, especially water on hot days.

With just a few sensible precautions, you should be able to
enjoy many rides off-road safe in the knowledge that you
will meet little if any traffic.

12 Sussex rides

*T*here couldn't be a better county than Sussex for riding a bike and enjoying the wonderful countryside, so here's a selection of rides that can be enjoyed at any time of the year.

All of them begin at railway stations, because some of them will be a fair distance from people's homes and not everyone has the use of a car or van to transport bikes. It is, in any case, more environmentally friendly to use the train, and often more enjoyable, too.

Most of the rides are circular, and some can be made circular with only a slight deviation from the route. For those who have come by car, it is always possible to take the train back to the original starting point.

Nearly every ride is between 10 and 20 miles long. Anything much less wouldn't be much of a ride at all (don't forget that your average speed is likely to be 5–10mph) and anything more might be considered too tough by many readers of this book.

Most rides are on quiet roads, but in some of them there are stretches (usually short) on thoroughfares which are rather busy. This is unavoidable in such a crowded county.

A few are off-road in places so that riders can sample the joy of bridleways and great tracks such as the South Downs Way. The rides vary from those on the flat to a couple with some extremely testing hills – but these are well worth the ascent.

The directions have been made as simple as possible and there are clear route maps, but it's always worth taking an Ordnance Survey map with you in case of any difficulty.

Each ride contains a brief description of the course and its length; directions to the starting point; an outline of the route with an idea of the terrain; a brief guide to shops and refreshments on route; and a thumbnail sketch of local places of interest.

Happy cycling!

1 A Ride to Devil's Dyke

9 miles
Portslade circular

This ride takes you along the urban fringes of Portslade and
Hove right up to the Devil's Dyke beauty spot and back. It is
short and can easily be accomplished on a summer's
evening – one of the best times for such a ride. It's hard
work getting there, but the views are stupendous and the
descent is glorious.

Getting there
Portslade Station is served by trains on the West Coastway
line from Brighton, Hove and Worthing. There is plenty of
parking in nearby roads.

Terrain
Some of the bridleways leading to the Dyke are rather
rutted, but both the Benfield Valley and Dyke Railway
cycleways are well paved. Hilly on the way to the Dyke;
steep downhill stretches on the way back.

Refreshments
Plenty in Portslade where there are pubs and cafes. More
drinks at Hangleton Manor and at the Dyke. On the way
back is the Downsman pub at the start of the Dyke Railway,
and a mile down the road is the Grenadier.

Shops
Good bike shop just north of Portslade station. Many other
shops in Boundary and Station Roads just south of station.
Sainsbury's store on the way.

Things to see
• Benfield Valley is an area being turned into a nature
reserve, noted especially for its glow-worms.

• Hangleton Manor (just off cycle path north of Sainsbury's) is now a pub and is the oldest domestic building in Hove.

• Foredown Tower (Brighton & Hove Council; admission charge) is a countryside centre with a camera obscura.

• Devil's Dyke (*above*) is a natural dry valley close to the scarp of the Downs, commanding views as far west as the Isle of Wight.

• The Dyke Railway (much of its route still evident) went all the way from Aldrington Halt to a point below the Dyke on one of the steepest gradients in the country. It closed just before the second world war.

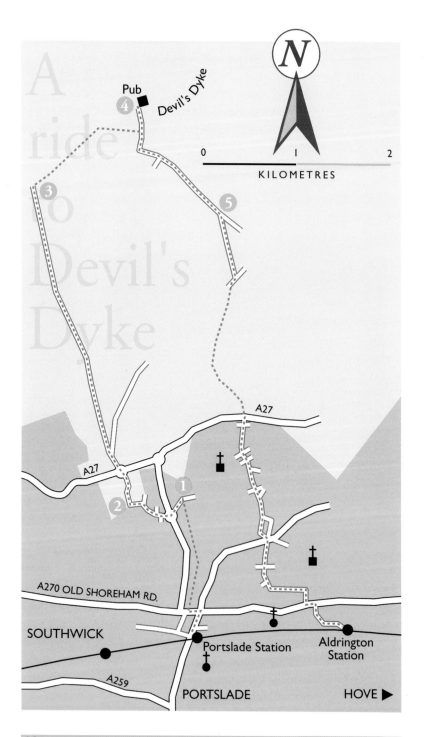

DIRECTIONS

Turn R out of Portslade Station heading north. Cross lights at Old Shoreham Road and ride down north pavement. Turn R after a few yards into Benfield Valley cycle path. Head north for a mile, passing Sainsbury's on your L and Hangleton Manor on your R.

At end of cycle path, turn left into Hangleton Lane [1] and after a few yards cross over roundabout with Hangleton Link Road. Continue into Fox Way and up steep hill. At top turn R into Foredown Road. [2]

Ignore Crest Way and continue straight along bridleway to Foredown Tower where there is a good map of the Downs in Hove. Cross Brighton bypass and immediately turn L up steep concrete path. Continue straight along level bridleway for more than a mile passing dew pond and triangulation point on R. Ignore all turns.

Path eventually becomes more grassy and starts rising until you come to a gate. Go through and turn sharp R [3], following blue bridleway rather than yellow footpath sign, and climb pleasant grassy track. At top pass through gate. Almost immediately fork R and take South Downs way to Devil's Dyke Road. Turn L and after a few yards you are at the Dyke. [4]

Now it's downhill all the way. Continue straight down Devil's Dyke Road, being careful at sharp bend and junction with road to Saddlescombe. After a mile, fork R down bridleway [5] towards Dyke Railway. Continue downhill then turn sharp R and L at Brighton and Hove Golf Club, going along old railway track and through gate. After a long mile the track ends.

Turn quickly L then R into Poplar Avenue and continue down steep hill to Westway. Turn L and veer R towards Grenadier roundabout. Here turn L into Elm Drive and continue down hill. At end turn R into Holmes Avenue, left into Old Shoreham Road (using crossing if preferred), and R into Amherst Crescent. At bottom of hill, turn R and you are at Aldrington Halt. To return to Portslade, another mile away, continue under railway arch down Tamworth Road and turn R into Portland Road. Station is at the end.

2 Bosham, Boats & Bracklesham Bay

15 miles
Start: Bosham; finish Chichester (or Bosham circular)
Unlike several other rides in this book, this one is over
entirely flat ground, making it easy going. There are
delightful sea and harbour views for much of the way. It can
be achieved only during the main boating season because
the little ferry at West Itchenor doesn't operate in the winter.

Getting there
Bosham Station is on the main West Coastway line with
regular services from Worthing and Brighton. There is
adequate parking nearby, and this could be converted into a
circular ride by returning to Bosham directly from the
finishing point at Chichester.

Terrain
Flat all the way, and therefore easy on the legs. Most of the
ride is on roads but the approach to the ferry can be slippery
at low tide. The canal towpath is rideable at all seasons.

Refreshments
Plenty of pubs at Bosham, and more at West Itchenor, East
Wittering, Hunston and Chichester. Teas, ice creams and a
fish restaurant at East Wittering. Restaurants and cafes to
suit all tastes at Chichester.

Shops
A few in Bosham, as well as at East Wittering and
Bracklesham. A full range of shopping (including a cycle
shop) at Chichester.

Things to see
• Bosham is a splendid boating village and is reputed to be
the place where King Canute tried to turn back the tide
(although the evidence is lacking). Every year, unwary

motorists suffer the indignity of finding their cars submerged by water.

● East Wittering and Bracklesham are two of the best small coastal resorts in Sussex with plenty of sand at low tide. West Wittering, well worth a detour, is even better.

● Earnley Gardens (admission charge) offer an eccentric but engaging mixture of attractions, appealing to adults and children alike.

● The Chichester Canal is the link between the city and the harbour. It is being restored slowly, and the section with the cycle track is fully navigable. You can hire boats or take a motor boat trip in the summer.

● Chichester is the county town of West Sussex. Its dominant cathedral can be seen from many points on the ride. The city also has walls which can be walked in places. Its other attractions include the Festival Theatre and Pallant House Gallery (admission charge).

The village of Bosham, on the edge of Chichester Harbour.

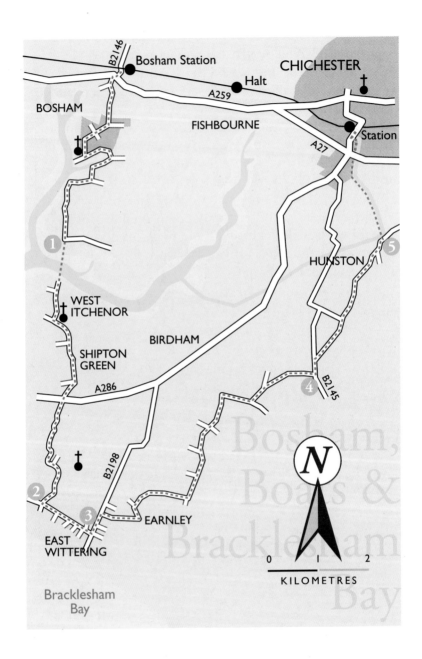

DIRECTIONS

Turn L out of Bosham Station and cross straight over at roundabout. At the next roundabout, turn R and head towards Bosham. Once there, go straight on down Bosham Lane to water's edge and then turn L. This road gets covered at high tide, when it is best to use the nearby footpath.

Follow the road right round the picturesque harbour and turn R into Shore Road. Where the road turns sharp L,[1] keep straight on down the footpath following the sign to the ferry.

The spire of Chichester Cathedral can be seen for miles around.

The ferry itself is small, frequent and extremely effective. The cost per yard makes it one of the dearest crossings in the country but the alternative detour would be many miles.

After the crossing to West Itchenor, carry straight on past Ship Inn and through Shipton Green[2] towards East Wittering going across the A286. At East Wittering, turn L unless you want to take a peek at the village and visit the beach.

At Bracklesham, turn L again[3] (R if you want to visit the splendid shoreline) and soon afterwards turn R past thatched cottage into Clappers Lane. Turn L at Earnley and soon afterwards turn R, following sign to Sidlesham. Pass Earnley Gardens and go through Almodington with its glasshouses until, at junction by white cottage, turn R into Mapsons Lane. Soon afterwards, turn L.

At the Selsey road, turn L on to main road[4] and head towards Chichester for more than a mile. Follow signs to Hunston and pass the Spotted Cow. Just after roundabout, turn L at a blue public footpath sign,[5] cross canal bridge and cycle down towpath.

This delightful last lap also has the huge advantage of going under the Chichester bypass rather than negotiating one of its many roundabouts. At canal basin join road turn R and Chichester Station is in front of you.

3 From Polegate to Pevensey

18 miles
Start Polegate; finish Pevensey & Westham

This ride uses the Cuckoo Trail on a former railway line and is one of the best cycle tracks in the south. It later goes on mainly quiet roads through woodland, and then across the open marshes of Pevensey. You would have to be mean-spirited indeed not to appreciate the varied beauty of the Sussex countryside here.

Getting there

Polegate Station is on the East Coastway line and accessible from Brighton, Lewes, Haywards Heath, Eastbourne and Hastings. There is parking nearby at weekends. The route can easily be made into a circular ride.

Terrain

The Cuckoo Trail has a good surface all the way. There is one short stretch of rough track on leaving the trail. After that the route is on minor roads. There are a couple of hills between the trail and the marsh, but otherwise this ride is pretty flat.

Refreshments

Pubs at Polegate, Hailsham, Hellingly and Pevensey. Cafes and restaurants at Polegate and Hailsham, and at Old Loom Mill between the two.

Shops

Plenty of basic shopping available in both Polegate and Hailsham, but not a lot after that until the end of the ride. Cycle shop usefully placed on route in Polegate.

Things to see

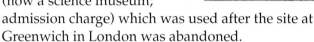

- The Cuckoo Trail is an ideal introduction to off-road cycling and was built by the cycle track charity Sustrans. It has witty sculptures at various points along the route.
- Herstmonceux, just off the route, has the fine observatory (now a science museum; admission charge) which was used after the site at Greenwich in London was abandoned.
- Pevensey has the historic castle (English Heritage; admission charge to central keep) and marshes which are among the most extensive in the county.

The Roman west gateway of Pevensey Castle.

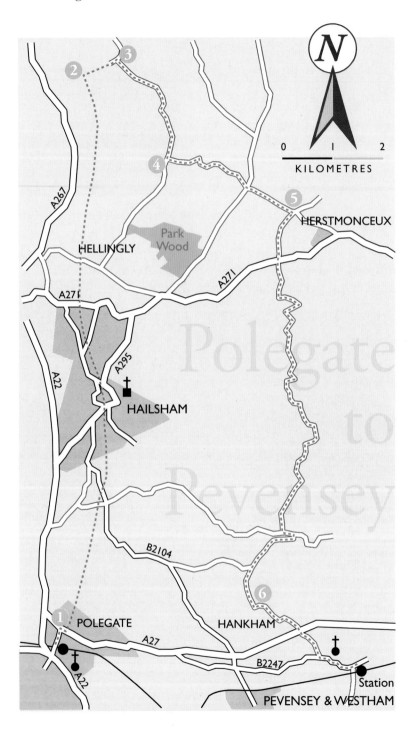

DIRECTIONS

Turn R out of Polegate Station and R again shortly afterwards into main road. Soon after turn L into School Lane and join the Cuckoo Trail.[1]

Follow the well signposted trail heading north noting two special cycle crossings over roads. Most of the track is on the old railway line between Polegate and Heathfield but there are two short diversions through housing estates, one of which brings you past Hailsham Common Pond.

Pass through Hailsham and Hellingly where you can still see the old railway station, now a house. Continue for a couple of miles towards Horam but before you get there, note that you are passing under some pylons. Just after that, turn R through gate[2] down rough track and turn R into minor road.[3]

Pevensey Marshes are both ecologically important and hauntingly beautiful.

Climb Grove Hill and at top turn L into the narrow and charming Cinderford Lane.[4] After short steep hill, go straight over crossroads towards Herstmonceux. Take first R[5] and soon afterwards, cross the A271, taking care.

Turn L again towards Herstmonceux and then R towards Pevensey down long narrow lane across marshes. Turn L at T junction,[6] again towards Pevensey and then R towards Hankham. Go straight on at T junction. Here it is possible to complete a circular tour and head back towards Polegate by turning R and following 'Route 2' signs until you reach the Cuckoo Trail again. For those not doing so, turn L after school sign and ride over A27. Continue straight on to Westham. Turn L into main road and R to Pevensey and Westham station.

4 Along the Forest Way

20 miles
East Grinstead circular

Here's a lovely rural ride in the north of the county. It goes along the Forest Way, an old railway track, from East Grinstead to Groombridge. Returning, the route goes through attractive Sussex villages such as Hartfield, known for its connection with A.A.Milne. The journey could take an afternoon or be stretched out to cover a full day. The ride can also be combined with the Worth Way (*see page 30*) to make a complete round trip of 36 miles.

Getting there
East Grinstead station is accessible from London and will eventually be the northern terminus of the Bluebell Railway from Sheffield Park. It is on the A22 London to Eastbourne road. There is parking at the station, and pay-and-display parking in the town centre.

Terrain
The Forest Way has a generally good surface and the gradients are generally gentle, but large shallow puddles can form after heavy rain. You can go straight back along it if you wish, but the journey by road is full of interest, if a bit busy. There are a few hills, but nothing to worry about.

Refreshments
Pubs, restaurants and cafes abound in East Grinstead, which is just as well since there is rather a long gap after that. There are pubs at Withyham, Hartfield and Forest Row, while Hartfield also has tea rooms.

Shops
All you could possibly want in East Grinstead, including a cycle shop. Pooh souvenir shop in Hartfield. Groceries are available in Forest Row.

Things to see

- East Grinstead is an ancient market town with a fine High Street dating back to the 14th century.
- Ashdown House, just north of Forest Row, was built for Lord Heathfield in 1795 by Benjamin Latrobe who is much better known for designing the White House in Washington.
- The River Medway can be seen for much of the Forest Way, which follows its valley. Rising in the Weald, the Medway emerges 70 miles further on in the Thames estuary.
- Withyham is mentioned in the Domesday Book, and four of the farms are still operating today. It has an imposing church.
- Forest Way Country Park follows the line of the disused railway. It was bought by East Sussex County Council in 1971.
- Hartfield is known for Winnie the Pooh. Just to the west can be found Pooh Bridge where the game of Poohsticks was played.
- Forest Row, once a series of lodges to house royal hunting parties going to nearby Ashdown Forest, became a coaching halt before being a railway village. Now it is a stopping-off place for motorists on the A22, and a thriving village in its own right.

Sackville College.

DIRECTIONS

Leave East Grinstead Station through car park and cross straight over roundabout on to Railway Approach, walking the last section against the one-way system. Turn R into the busy London Road and L at a mini roundabout down the historic High Street. Continue past Sackville College.

At roundabout, note Beeching Way, named after Dr Richard Beeching, appointed by the Macmillan government to reduce the railway system. He lived at East Grinstead and even cut the line to his own town.

Cross over main road just before roundabout to R side of the road and turn R on to the Forest Way[1] and into the charming country park. Cross minor road and continue until you descend short steep slope to cross the busy A22.[2] Continue on long straight stretch of old track. At Hartfield Station turn L then R. Cross Beech Green Lane (with a gate on each side) and pass Withyham Station. After another short steep descent you are on the B2188 road. Turn L if you want to look at the attractive village of Groombridge. Otherwise turn R and climb hill.[3]

Enjoy the dazzling descent into Withyham and continue on the B2110 towards Hartfield.[4] Follow road signs to Forest Row, keeping on B2110. At Forest Row, turn R on to A22. Just after crossing two low stone bridges, turn L back on to the Forest Way and return the way you came to East Grinstead.

The Tudor Bookshop in East Grinstead High Street has an unusual cork inlay.

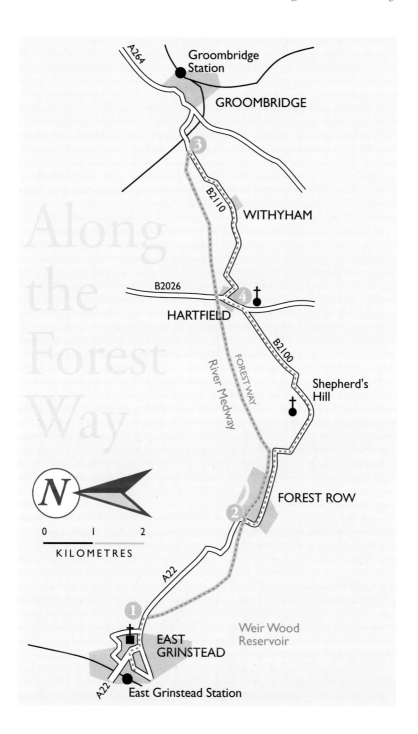

5 High on the South Downs Way

15 miles
Falmer circular

The South Downs Way is one of the few long-distance paths in Britain where cyclists are allowed as well as ramblers. This wonderful airy ride is an excellent introduction to it, as we meet one of its fairly flat stretches. We also encounter it again briefly towards the end of the ride.

Getting there

The ride starts and ends at Falmer Station, which is on the East Coastway line directly accessible from Brighton, Eastbourne, Hastings and Seaford. It could also be done from Lewes station with little deviation. There is parking in several places at Stanmer Park, just off the A27 north of Brighton, for cyclists arriving by car or van.

Terrain

Most of this ride is off-road, but is usually pretty firm on all but the wettest days. It is a hilly ride, with a long climb up to Ditchling Beacon and another sharp ascent after Kingston, but there are some long and glorious downhill stretches.

Refreshments

Pubs at Falmer, Lewes, Kingston and Woodingdean. Lewes has several good restaurants. There are teas and ice creams, plus more besides at the Stanmer Stores, and there is often an ice cream van in the car park at Ditchling Beacon.

Shops

Plenty for almost all needs at Lewes, cycle shop included. Not much else on the main part of ride.

Things to see

• Sussex University. Original buildings designed by Sir Basil Spence are now listed on this 1960s campus.

A rooftop view from School Hill in Lewes towards Malling Down.

- Stanmer Park. This large estate was sold to Brighton Council soon after the last war by the Earl of Chichester and is the nearest piece of proper country to Brighton. The house is being restored, and there is a small country museum next door. In Stanmer village there is a working farm.
- The Chattri is a memorial to the Indian soldiers who died while convalescing at Brighton during the First World War. It can be reached by footpaths.
- Ditchling Beacon is the highest point on the East Sussex Downs: wonderful views over the Weald.
- Lewes, the county town of East Sussex, has a castle, several fine old churches and the Barbican and Anne of Cleves House museums. Thomas Paine, who inspired the French and American revolutions, lived here.
- Kingston is a delightful small village much favoured by university folk.
- Falmer is bisected by the A27 and too close to the A27 for comfort, but has a pleasing church and pond.
- Castle Hill National Nature Reserve is surprisingly remote considering its location near Woodingdean, and is a fine example of chalk downland.

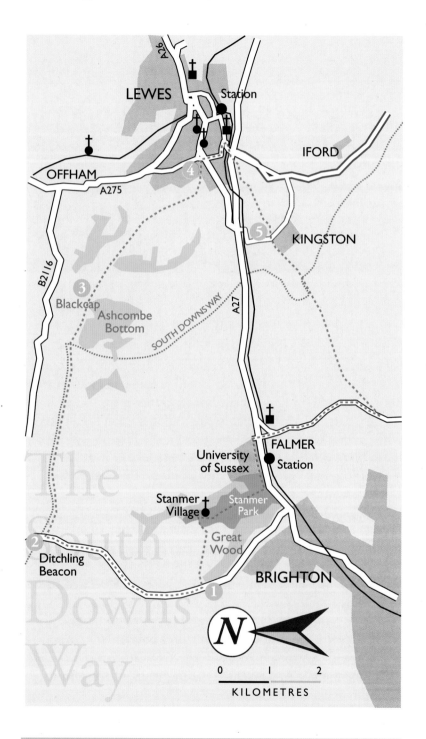

DIRECTIONS

Leave Falmer Station and take the subway to Sussex University under the A27 – you can easily see where it goes as you approach from the top. Emerge on the campus and turn sharp L on to cycle track running parallel with the main road. Where the track joins a small road after a few hundred yards, turn R through lodge gates into Stanmer Park.

Ride on park road past house on the L. Turn R at church and quickly L into village. Turn L at pond and go through gate on to hilly minor road marked as bridleway. At top of steep hill, pass by more lodges out of park and turn R into Ditchling Beacon Road.[1]

By dew pond on L, observe the Chattri memorial about a mile away to the west. Carry on up the hill to Ditchling Beacon. Opposite car park turn R on to South Downs Way.[2] Continue straight on following markers until you get to Blackcap.[3]

Again, press forward on to grass track to reach triangulation point on top of hill. Then follow main track down the hill heading towards the buildings of the old Lewes racecourse. Continue ahead down well marked but narrow bridleway down the hill, always keeping the course on your R. This path become a rough track shortly before meeting main road.

Turn R and go straight over Lewes Prison crossroads[4] into Winterbourne Hollow down steep hill. Turn R at roundabout and immediately R again into Juggs Road. Continue on this high ancient highway, crossing the lane to Kingston village[5] into Kingston Ridge following red markers.

Soon after passing through a gate at start of remarkably steep hill, take R fork and continue pushing upwards. Keep going straight on as you rejoin South Downs Way. But where the way turns off to the R, ignore that and continue straight on towards large transmitter mast at Woodingdean, passing Castle Hill nature reserve on the L.

At Falmer Road, turn R and scoot down hill to the village. Turn L on to short stretch of A27 to reach the station or continue over bridge and turn L on other side to reach cycle track if you are returning to Stanmer Park.

6 A Ride in the Adur Valley

9 miles
Shoreham circular

Shoreham is a wonderful place to start bikes rides. It is a small town with a good rail service, and the Coastal Link, which quickly takes you to both the South Downs Way and the Downs Link long distance routes. This pleasant ride takes you into the old town of Steyning on either side of the River Adur.

Ship's prow outside the Crown & Anchor, Shoreham.

Getting there
Shoreham Station is easily reached by rail from Chichester Worthing, Brighton, Hove and Haywards Heath. There is parking by the station, and at weekends it is also available in many of the side streets nearby.

Terrain
The Coastal Link, South Downs Way and Downs Link are all generally in good condition, but can become slightly muddy after heavy rain. The rest of the ride is on minor roads and well-maintained footpaths. Flat until Bramber, then a series of hills – some steep but none huge.

Refreshments
Plenty of pubs at Shoreham, Bramber and Steyning. All three also have good restaurants and cafes. Shoreham Airport has a bar and restaurant.

Shops
Good selection (including cycle shops) at Shoreham and Steyning. Supermarkets bigger in Shoreham.

Things to see

- St Mary de Haura church in Shoreham and St Nicolas Church at Old Shoreham are well worth a visit, as are St Andrew's Church at Steyning and the tiny churches of Coombes and Botolphs.
- The Marlipins Museum (Sussex Archaeological Socety) and Steyning Museum (both admission charges) are local museums of great interest.
- Bramber Castle (English Heritage; free entry) is a ruin and a wonderful place for a picnic.
- Shoreham Airport is one of the oldest in the country, starting in 1910. The restaurant offers excellent views of the light aircraft coming and going.
- Lancing College has a chapel with a magnificent rose window. It can be visited and is free.
- Coombes Farm is run on ecological principles and is open to the public at times during the season (admission charge).

Shoreham, looking towards the bridge.

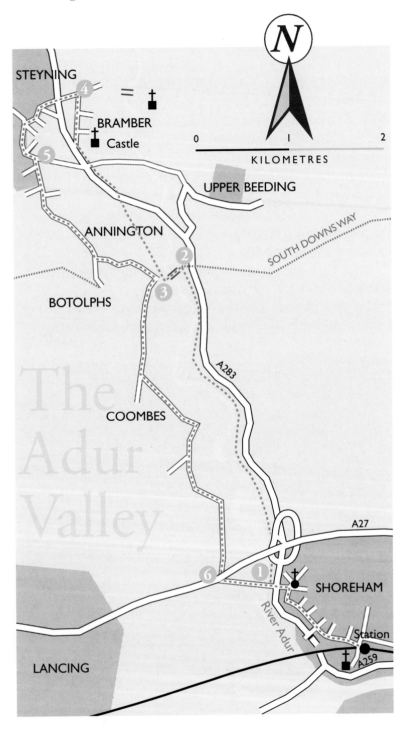

DIRECTIONS

Leave Shoreham Station and head north before immediately
turning L into Queen's Place. Continue straight on over three
minor junctions into Swiss Gardens. You do not have right of way
at the first and third.

Carry on into Connaught Avenue and after half a mile turn L
into Upper Shoreham Road. At nearby roundabout mount far
pavement and head north before immediately turning L towards
old toll bridge. At railway track a few yards ahead, turn R on to
Coastal Link.[1]

Keep river on L for two miles, following the path, until you
meet bridge over the Adur and the South Downs Way. Turn L on
to bridge[2] and turn R after crossing it. Follow South Downs Way
for short distance to junction with Downs Link and then turn R
on to Downs Link.[3] The ride can be shortened at this point by
carrying straight on into the Coombes Road and turning L.

Take care while crossing Steyning bypass and immediately turn
L, keeping parallel to the road. At roundabout, cross The Street
into Castle Lane and go straight on into Roman Road. Ignore
Downs Link turn off to R and continue up hill. At top opposite
Castle Way, turn L on to footpath and walk if desired.[4] Continue
on high footbridge over Steyning bypass and carry straight on into
Holland Road. Keep going straight on to another footpath down a
hill and past the Steyning Centre on your L.

Turn L into Church Street and at nearby junction with High
Street, turn L again but R if you want to have a proper look at
Steyning. After short downhill stretch, climb small hill and ignore
first turning on R for Sompting via the Bostal. Immediately after,
turn R into Maudlin Lane.[5] Continue straight on into Annington
Lane and Botolphs Road, cycling through the pretty hamlets of
those names.

Continue through Coombes to junction with A27. At traffic
lights,[6] turn R and then immediately L past Shoreham Airport and
over old toll bridge. You are now back at the Coastal Link and
continue your way to Shoreham Station the way you came via
Connaught Avenue.

7 Over the Hills to West Hoathly

20 miles
Haywards Heath circular

If you ever thought the Sussex Weald was flat, you will think again after this tough circular ride from Haywards Heath to West Hoathly, which just touches Ashdown Forest. Admittedly this is the High rather than the Low Weald, but the hills are sharp and plentiful. You may not be surprised, after some climbing, to find at the mid-point of the ride that you are as high as on parts of the South Downs, which can usually be seen shimmering in the distance.

Getting there

Haywards Heath is amply served by trains from London, Brighton, Eastbourne and from most places along the west coast. There is a station car park, and the ride can also be started about half a mile to the east, where there is parking on nearby roads.

Terrain

The whole ride is on metalled roads. Hills for much of the way, especially between West Hoathly and Ardingly. The

ride is generally uphill to Ashdown Forest and easier on the way back. Some of the roads can be rather busy on weekdays but all, even the A275, are acceptable at weekends.

Old Place, Lindfield.

Refreshments
Pubs, restaurants and cafes galore at Haywards Heath. More pubs at Lindfield, Horsted Keynes, Danehill, Chelwood Common, Sharpthorne, West Hoathly, Ardingly and at Avins Bridge south of Ardingly College.

Shops
Plenty, including supermarkets and a cycle shop, at Haywards Heath. Sparse otherwise. Souvenirs available at Ashdown Forest visitor centre.

Typical Ashdown Forest view.

Things to see
• The Bluebell Railway, which runs from Sheffield Park through Horsted Keynes to Kingscote, will eventually link with British Rail at East Grinstead. It was one of the first privately-owned steam railways in Britain and is one of the most popular. (Admission charge.)

• Ashdown Forest is one of the largest in southern England. The forest centre (free), which is the goal of this ride, gives plenty of information about its history and about the nature trails which you can follow. Almost opposite, the Ashdown Park Hotel occasionally opens its extensively landscaped grounds to the public.

• The Priest House at West Hoathly (Sussex Archaeological Society; admission charge) is a former yeoman's home, its displays giving an intriguing reminder of the simple lives of yesteryear.

• Ardingly College (not open to the public) is one of three public schools founded by the Rev Nathaniel Woodard.

• Ardingly Reservoir (free) is a tranquil spot for walking or picnics.

• Borde Hill (admission charge) is one of the great landscaped gardens of Sussex.

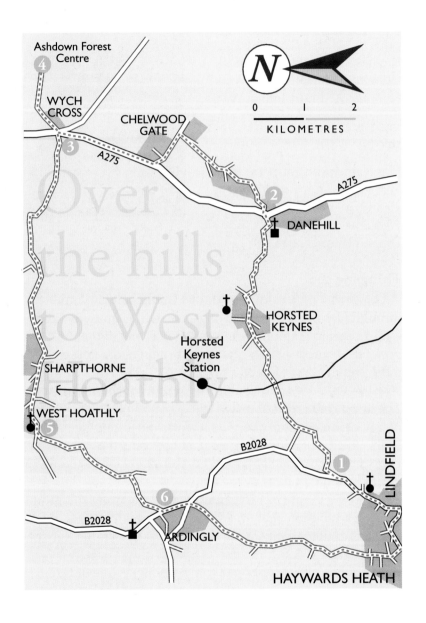

DIRECTIONS

Turn R out of station and at nearby junction head straight on towards Lindfield, ignoring all diversions on this road. Continue past the pond through the picture postcard village and climb a hill. After descending the other side and crossing the River Ouse, turn R on to minor road. [1]

Follow signs to Horsted Keynes, again ignoring tempting lanes on either side, and go under Bluebell Railway to pass through the wealthy and well kept village. Soon after, fork R for Danehill. Just before reaching the busy A275, take L fork along short one-way street and cross with care heading towards Chelwood Common. [2]

After riding through this village turn L at T junction and then right on to A275 for unavoidable but short stretch of main road. After a mile, join the A22 and immediately afterwards at Wych Cross traffic lights, turn R. [3] After another mile, stop for well-earned rest at Ashdown Forest Centre on the L and admire the rolling views to the north. [4]

Head back the way you came and this time cross straight over at Wych Cross on to minor road which runs along ridge with great glimpses of the Downs to the L. Head towards and then through the pleasant but unremarkable village of Sharpthorne to West Hoathly. [5] Once there turn L where there is a sign to the church and head through the unspoilt village.

The Priest House, West Hoathly.

Hurtle down narrow lane, taking care of any approaching cars, for one of the best and scariest descents in Sussex. Where the long downhill stretch ends, you will almost certainly have to walk up a one in five gradient to the B2028. Turn L towards Ardingly. [6]

At the village, turn R following signs towards the College and carry straight on towards Haywards Heath. Rejoin road from Lindfield and return to the station.

8 A Glide Through Glynde

19 miles
Lewes circular (or from Glynde)

This is a delightful ride from the East Sussex county town of Lewes, through the almost feudal village of Glynde, round the back of Ringmer and into the splashy splendours of Barcombe Mills before exploring the hidden away hamlet of Hamsey. It avoids most main roads and is never far away from a watering hole. It can be ridden at any time of the year, and can take anything from a couple of hours to a whole day.

Clock tower, Glynde Place.

Getting there
By rail to Lewes station, where there is also parking. Lewes has a regular service from Brighton, Eastbourne, Seaford and Haywards Heath. The ride can also be done from Glynde.

Terrain
Generally undulating, with a few flat stretches. No really serious hills, but a couple of sharp rises followed by gentle glides. Most of the ride is on metalled roads and cycle tracks, apart from two stretches of rougher track each around a mile long.

Refreshments
Pubs at Lewes, Glynde, Ringmer, Barcombe and Offham. Cafes and restaurants at Lewes and Barcombe Mills.

Shops
Plenty of food shopping (including a Tesco supermarket right near the end of the route), and cycle shops in Lewes.

Lewes Castle.

Things to see
● Lewes has the castle, the Barbican House Museum and Anne of Cleves House museum (all Sussex Archaeological Society; admission charge), Harvey's Brewery (tours by arrangement), several fine churches and the Priory ruins.

● Glynde has Glynde Place, the home of Viscount Hampden, which is open during the summer (admission charge). Nearby is the celebrated Glyndebourne Opera House.

● Barcombe Mills has pleasant riverside walks and the old station (now a restaurant). Boats are available for hire in season at the Anchor Inn.

● The Pells in Lewes is one of the largest and oldest open-air swimming pools in the country. It is open during the summer for a refreshing dip (admission charge).

DIRECTIONS

Turn R out of Lewes Station and at first junction turn hard R again going back in the direction you came from but down towards the station car park. Do not enter car park but turn L. At junction, turn R and walk against one way system a few yards to roundabout. Turn R and follow serpentine road round to Cliffe High Street.

Turn R into Cliffe High Street over bridge crossing River Ouse and continue to end of road. Turn R into South Street and at the end follow path parallel to road.

Cross over just before large sign at approaching roundabout and take path, which quickly becomes a road, into the surprisingly pleasing hamlet of Southerham. Follow it R up short sharp hill to join A27. Turn L on to cycle track and follow this until a sign pointing L to Ranscombe Lane. [1]

After a mile of pleasant cycling up and down hills, sweep into Glynde and turn L at junction. [2] Climb sharp hill passing Glynde Place on R. At the next junction go straight on towards Ringmer and pass Glyndebourne Opera House.

Just before meeting the main road through Ringmer, turn R into Gote Lane by a 30mph sign. [3] Follow this road round until it becomes Harrisons Lane. At the end cross the main road, taking care.

At junction turn L and then quickly R towards Uckfield ignoring road to Norlington. On meeting A26, cross straight over on to footpath and turn R into minor road. Turn L into A 26 by sign for The Cock pub and endure 300 yards of busy traffic.

Thankfully, turn L towards Barcombe and head down pleasant, quiet road. Just after car park, turn R at fork and wheel bike along track over a series of bridges at Barcombe Mills. After the old toll bridge, turn L on to metalled lane and rejoin road.

After only a few yards, turn R opposite Barcombe Mills Station[4] down bridleway called Anchor Lane which follows the route of the former Lewes to Uckfield railway line.

At the end, turn R if you want to have a drink at the Anchor Inn, overlooking the river, which also offers boating in the summer.[5] Otherwise turn L up narrow lane with passing places. Follow this round bends for a mile and then turn L towards Barcombe.

At roundabout in Barcombe, go straight ahead towards Barcombe Mills but at next junction turn R towards Hamsey. Follow this narrow lane for two miles, always taking turns to Hamsey and then Offham.[6]

Cross Lewes–Haywards Heath railway line and, when almost at the A275 at Offham, turn L on to public right of way.

Continue on this track into Landport Road and carry straight on to path which quickly becomes a road again. Turn L down footpath and

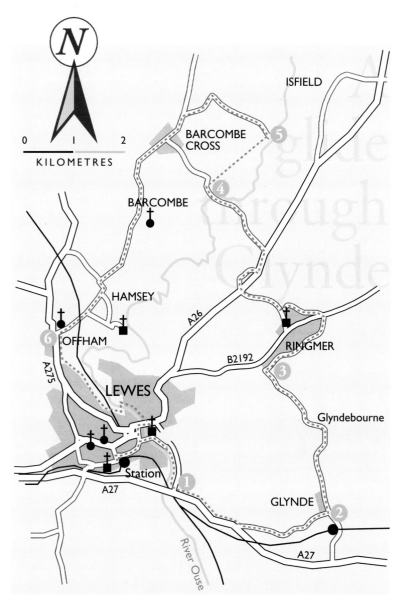

walk over railway bridge to join another road by the Pells lake in Lewes. Follow the lake round to the L and continue past the Pells open-air swimming pool (which is well worth a summer dip) over the Ouse on a pedestrian bridge. Turn R on to shared cycle and pedestrian paths by river, and follow signs all the way into Cliffe High Street. Turn R and retrace route to Lewes Station.

9 Worth Riding

16 miles
Three Bridges circular

This ride uses the whole length of the Worth Way on an old railway track between Three Bridges and East Grinstead. It returns along roads, or you can simply come back the same way. Although Crawley is full of new houses and you are only 30 miles from London, it's somehow possible to forget about all that for most of the journey.

Getting there

Three Bridges is on the main London to Brighton line. It can also be reached from Crawley, Horsham and the Arun Valley line. With just one change, it is accessible also from Eastbourne and Worthing. By road it is just off the A23.

Parking nearby, particularly at weekends.

Terrain

For much of its length the Worth Way has a hard surface, which is generally good even after heavy rain. The rest of the route is on roads. The Way itself is largely off-road. From East Grinstead, the road can be busy at times, although not excessively so. The old railway track is pretty flat, but the way back is undulating – and Turners Hill lives up to the latter part of its name.

Refreshments

Plenty in Three Bridges and East Grinstead, including pub, cafes and restaurants. Pubs at Crawley Down and Turners Hill. Teas available at Standen and at Tulley's.

Shops

Most of what anyone could desire at both Crawley and East Grinstead, which both have cycle shops. Some shopping at Crawley Down, and groceries at Turners Hill.

Worth is one of the finest Saxon churches in Britain.

Things to see

- Worth Church is one of the oldest in Sussex, dating from Saxon times, and the more modern Abbey (a school) is only just off the route.
- The Sussex Border Path, which forms part of the route, is 150 miles long and is well marked.
- East Grinstead has a fine but busy high street, with many buildings going back to the 14th Century.
- Standen (National Trust; admission charge) is a 19th century house with fine gardens and associations with William Morris.
- Saint Hill Manor nearby is the home of the Scientologists.
- The Bluebell Railway (admission charge) runs south from Kingcote through Horsted Keynes to Sheffield Park. It was one of the first privately operated steam railways in the country and will eventually be extended to East Grinstead.
- Tulley's Farm usually boasts a huge maze (admission charge) made out of maize in the summer. It also has a fruit-picking farm and a shop.

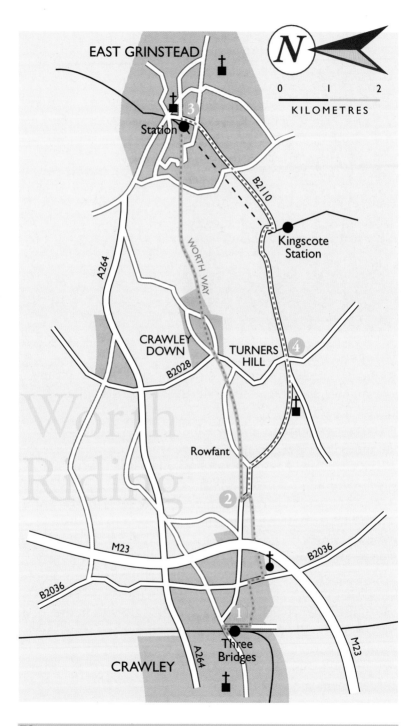

DIRECTIONS

Turn R out of Three Bridges station and walk along the pavement rather than cross the road, for after going under the line you immediately turn R into Station Hill, following blue marker signs. The road has a bike lane and traffic calming. Turn L soon after and you are on the Worth Way. [1]

After bridge under Balcombe Road, turn sharp R and then L before turning R on to minor road and L on to a track again. Continue past Worth Church and over the M23 passing from ancient to modern in a few yards. Here the surface changes but is still good.

Go through gate at Rowfant and resist temptation to carry straight on down road. Instead turn sharp L and then quickly R to follow track again. [2] Cross Wallage Lane twice and Rowfant Station and go under Turners Hill road to Crawley Down, where you come to some shops.

Carry straight on and then turn R into Woodland Drive and then L into Hazel Way. Follow on into Cob Close and straight on past lake. Go under two bridges and you are at East Grinstead. Ride through the car park and wheel your bike over a footbridge to the station. [3]

Summer house at the end of the upper terrace, Standen.

Turn R out of station and follow the B2110 towards Turners Hill. Turn R at roundabout and up hill towards Standen before going straight across junction. Continue past sign to Kingscote (where the Bluebell Railway currently ends) and continue towards Turners Hill, looking at South Downs to L and North Downs to R.

Continue over village crossroads [4] and soon afterwards fork R towards Crawley, noting Tulley's farm shop. On sharp bend just after sign denoting horses continue straight on and rejoin Worth Way. Retrace your original route to Three Bridges.

10 Woodland Way to Chichester

17 miles
Start Ford; finish Chichester

This is a delightful ride, largely through woods, from the village of Ford on the edge of the Downs to Chichester. It is one of the few in this book not capable of being made into a circular route, but people arriving by car can take their bikes back to the starting point by train. It is a lovely ride at any time of year, but particularly pleasant in the autumn.

Getting there
Ford station is on the West Coastway line and is accessible from Brighton, Hove, Worthing and Chichester. There is a car park at the station.

Terrain
Fairly flat, apart from rises between Slindon and Eartham. The first bridleway can be very muddy in wet weather. The Centurion Way is paved and is in excellent condition. All roads are in good order. Short stretches are rather busy, but most are quiet.

Refreshments
Pubs at Ford, Binsted, Slindon, Eartham, Halnaker, Lavant and Chichester. Every kind of cafe and restaurant in the county town itself. Tea rooms near Binsted.

Shops
The complete works, including supermarket and a cycle shop, in Chichester. Very little otherwise on the route.

Things to see
• Arundel (one mile from route) has a cathedral, castle (admission charge), lake and wildfowl centre (Wildfowl Trust, admission charge).

- Slindon. Delightful large village surrounded by National Trust woodland. The Nore folly can be reached on foot.
- Boxgrove Priory (near Halnaker) dates from the 12th century. Not far away 'Boxgrove Man' was found – dating from half a million years ago, and the earliest human yet discovered in Europe.
- Halnaker windmill (restored shell of the building open to view). Worth the detour if only for the views.
- Goodwood House (admission charge). Seat of the Duke of Richmond with fine collection of paintings. The estate also has the famous racecourse, a golf centre, a motoring racing circuit and an aerodrome – all close to this ride.
- Centurion Way. Part of the old railway north of Chichester, converted into a cycle track by Sustrans.
- Chichester. County town of West Sussex with cathedral, Pallant House art gallery (admission charge), Festival Theatre and walls you can walk.

The gothick splendour of Arundel Castle is just off the route of this ride.

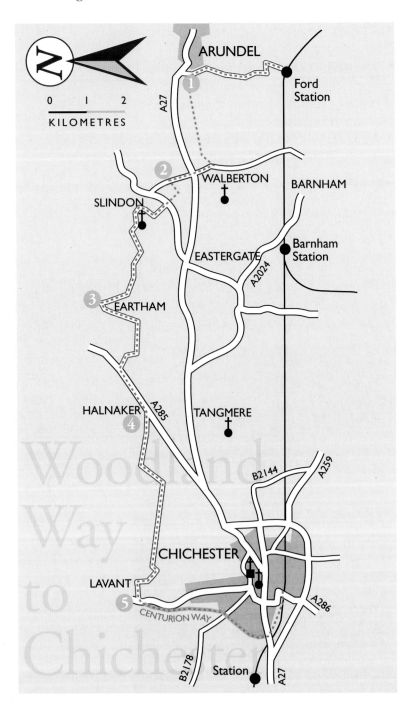

DIRECTIONS

Turn L out of station and continue towards Arundel before turning L again into winding Tortington Lane. Continue heading north with great glimpses of the cathedral and castle at Arundel.

Just before A 27, turn sharp L towards Binsted and a few yards down the hill turn R [1] on to the bridleway through woodland. Continue on this for more than a mile ignoring all tempting footpaths to the side. Eventually it emerges by the side of a field.

Turn L towards Binsted again and, just before the Black Horse, turn sharp R towards Yapton. Turn R again towards Slindon just past the Beam Ends tea rooms. Be extremely careful crossing the A27 dual carriageway by Oats brasserie.

At a T junction sign, turn L down well marked, grassy bridleway on to the National Trust Slindon estate. [2] Go through gate and turn R and cross the busy A29 with care. Continue up School Hill and pass the Newburgh Arms into Top Road. Carry on past Catholic Church and Slindon College to descend a welcome hill.

Start rising again and turn R towards Eartham at T junction. [3] At the George Inn, turn L and glide down hill toward Halnaker. Before reaching the bottom turn R, again with Halnaker in mind. Turn L on to busy A285 for short stretch and R at Halnaker itself, keeping the wall of the Goodwood estate on your R. [4]

At Goodwood House, turn L and then R at crossroads on to straight road towards Lavant. Keep going west at roundabout and at church turn L.

Soon after, fork R down no through road and climb on short stretch of bike track to main road. Cross straight over to footpath marked towards Centurion Way. Soon afterwards, reach the Way and turn L towards Chichester. [5]

You now have more than two miles on one of the best cycle paths in the country, going downhill gently all the way on an old railway track.

Where the track ends, continue into Westgate following signs to the city. Turn R before city centre on to a well-marked cycle track through playing field. Continue through subway into car park of Chichester Station.

11 In the Cuckmere Valley

12 miles
Berwick circular
This short ride goes through some of the most classic
country in southern England, centred on the upper reaches
of the Cuckmere Valley. There are attractions galore, and on
a clear day the views of the Downs are heart-stopping. It's
an ideal first ride for people trying out their cycling legs,
and can take anything from an hour to a day.

Getting there
The ride starts from Berwick station, which is on the East
Coastway line with access from Brighton, Lewes, Haywards
Heath, Eastbourne and Hastings. Trains call at this country
station hourly. There is parking at the station. An alternative
starting point for those arriving by car is at Wilmington
village, where there is a good car park with toilets.

Terrain
Generally excellent, even on the short stretch of bridleway
approaching Alfriston. The route is undulating with a few
flat stretches, and there are no enormous hills.

Refreshments
Surprisingly good for a short country ride. There are pubs at
Berwick station, Upper Dicker, Arlington, Wilmington,
Alfriston and Berwick. Crossways Hotel at the Wilmington
crossroads provides real gourmet food in the evenings, and
there are restaurants and cafes at Alfriston. Food of all kinds
is also available at Drusilla's, including some typically
Sussex and English dishes.

Shops
There are few on this ride except in Alfriston, where you
will find groceries and knick-knacks in abundance.

Things to see

- Arlington Reservoir, created in the 1970s, is a pleasant spot for a picnic and can also provide a circular walk of nearly two miles with plenty of bird life on view.
- St Bede's School (not open to the public) was the home of famous fraudster Horatio Bottomley, who was well loved by villagers for his generosity despite his many misdeeds.
- Michelham Priory (Sussex Archaeological Society; admission charge) is of medieval origin on a moated site, with the main building open to the public as well as the great barn, a water mill which makes flour and extensive planted grounds.
- Abbot's Wood is a square mile of woodland which can get muddy in winter. It has a picnic area, parking, a forest walk and a nature reserve.
- Wilmington has an ancient priory (not open to the public) and its churchyard has one of the largest yews in England.
- The Long Man of Wilmington is a mysterious figure and no one is quite sure of his origins. Originally made of chalk, he is now outlined in brick and is undeniably impressive.
- Lullington church is one of the smallest in Sussex – the remnant of a once-larger building. It is a great contrast with the fine church at Alfriston, known locally as the Cathedral of the Downs.
- Alfriston is a picture-postcard village – almost too popular on summer Sundays. It does boast Alfriston Clergy House (admission charge), the first property ever bought by the National Trust – for just £10.
- Drusilla's Zoo (admission charge) is a family attraction with many not very fierce animals, craft shops and plenty for children to do, including a large play area.
- The English Wine Centre just north of the zoo is what the name suggests and is open to the public.
- Berwick church is a historic building with wall paintings by members of the Bloomsbury set, including Duncan Grant and Vanessa Bell, whose country home was nearby at Charleston Farmhouse (admission charge).

DIRECTIONS

Turn L out of Berwick Station and head north, passing Arlington Reservoir on your R. Continue for a couple of miles to the village of Upper Dicker and turn R at pub by St Bede's School.[1] Continue past Michelham Priory on L and turn R at junction by Milton Hyde.

Carry on south with Abbot's Wood on your L and Old Oak Inn on your R. Ignore tempting turns to Arlington (unless you want to shorten the ride by half) and take L fork heading towards Polegate. Go over East Coastway line at level crossing and take care when heading straight across the busy A27[2] into Wilmington village past the Long Man pub.

Go past Priory with great views of the Long Man of Wilmington to the L, and rise to highest point on the ride where the road meets the South Downs Way. Then swoop down hill past Lullington Church. At the bottom, turn R towards Alfriston.[3]

On bend soon afterwards, turn L down bridleway and cross the Cuckmere on a bridge to emerge in Alfriston. Turn R into High Street and continue northwards past Drusilla's Zoo. Cross the

A27 at the round-about[4] and ride straight back to Berwick Station.

An alternative is to turn L just before Drusilla's to visit Berwick village with its church, and then turn R to cross the A27 and rejoin the main route.

The imposing 14th century gatehouse at Michelham Priory.

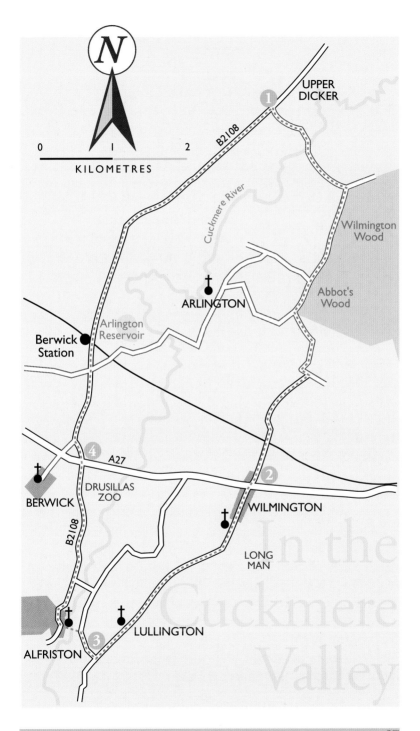

12 Enjoy It While You Can

11 miles
Christ's Hospital circular

Here's a ride in wooded countryside only a few miles from Horsham yet with a lovely rural atmosphere. Enjoy it while you can, for there are plans to build thousands of homes in

the Christ's Hospital area, so wrecking the tranquillity. It's an ideal ride for the novice – not too long or demanding, and along mainly peaceful paths or roads. A delight at any time of year, it's particularly pleasing in late spring or autumn.

Getting there

Christ's Hospital Station is on the Arun Valley line near Horsham. There is direct access from Chichester, Barnham and other stations on the line. People on the West Coastway line can reach it by changing at Barnham, while those on the Brighton line change at Three Bridges. There is parking at the station, but for those arriving by car Southwater Country Park might be a more convenient starting point.

Terrain

The Downs Link is a well-marked track. It can become wet with large shallow puddles in wet weather, but it is always negotiable. The private road is generally in reasonable condition at all times. The rest of the route follows well-maintained country lanes, usually with little traffic. Most of the terrain is flat, but there are one or two mild inclines.

Refreshments

There are pubs at Barns Green and Southwater, which also has a tea shop at the country park.

Shops

Make sure you stock up if you are starting at Christ's
Hospital, because there is no shop until Barns Green. There
is a reasonable array of shops at Southwater.

Things to see

● Christ's Hospital is the famous Bluecoat School which
moved out of London to give the youngsters a taste of the
countryside. It is not normally open to the public but has
extensive grounds.

● Barns Green is a beautiful village which hosts a popular
half marathon race each autumn when the leaves are at their
best. This ride uses part of the route.

● Southwater Country Park (*see page 91*) has a lake with
boating, and there are some pleasant walks nearby. It also
has a centre with exhibitions.

● The Downs Link
track is an old
railway line which
has been converted
into a bridleway and
cycle path.

Arches frame the quad at
Christ's Hospital School.

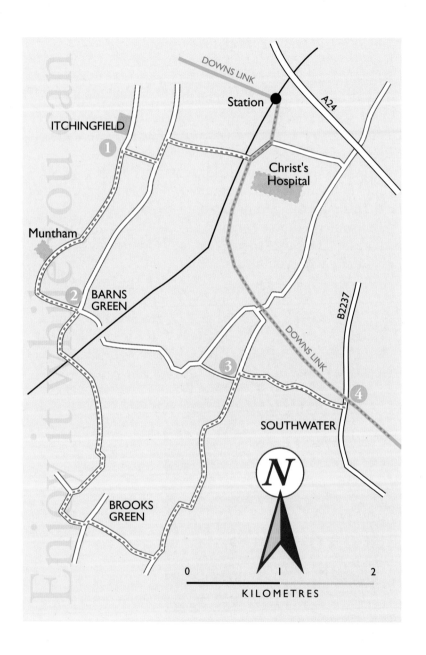

DIRECTIONS

Leave Christ's Hospital Station through the car park on the south side and use the road out, ignoring public footpath to the school. Fork R at first junction and follow road over railway bridge.

At T junction, turn L towards Barns Green, but after only a few yards turn R towards Itchingfield. After the village school, on sharp bend, turn L[1] down private road which is also a bridleway and follow this well marked track for about a mile, passing Muntham School on the way until the track becomes a road and you are in the delightful village of Barns Green.[2]

Turn R at village crossroads towards Brooks Green and go over level crossing down a wooded lane. Turn L at T junction towards Horsham and quickly R towards Dragons Green.

At T junction, turn L following sign to Southwater and L again at the next junction with the same destination in mind. Go past Marlpost Farm and turn R up Bonfire Hill.[3]

Eventually you arrive in Southwater and reach a crossroads. Do not go straight ahead down Andrew's Lane but take the short path just to the L towards Downs Link cycleway.[4] Turn R and continue until you arrive at Southwater Country Park.

After inspecting the park and possibly enjoying a cup of tea, go back the way you came on the Downs Link but this time stay on it and go through the old Southwater Station. Continue through field and on to track, always following the Downs Link symbols, until it runs parallel to the railway line and close to the school. On reaching the road, do not follow Downs Link but instead turn R and retrace your route to the station.

Southwater Country Park, created from a former brickworks.

Further afield

"Sussex has just
about everything the
cyclist can want,
but the time comes
when we feel the call
to be a little more
adventurous"

Sustrans
and the national cycle network

While the Dome at Greenwich was generally regarded as a failure, not all millennium projects were flops. One of the most successful has been the national cycle network – and it is by no means finished yet.

Armed with more than £40 million of National Lottery money, the cycle track building charity Sustrans (it stands for Sustainable Transport), opened half the route by the middle of 2000, with the intention of having 10,000 miles open by 2005.

This route will pass through or near most of the big cities and towns in the UK. A section of it will be within two miles of more than half the population. The network, both on quiet roads and on off-road tracks, will cater for cycle journeys involving work, school, pleasure and tourism.

Sustrans say the network is just a start in creating conditions that will attract people back to cycling and provide the spur for many further links and extensions. It has liaised with more than 400 organisations, including councils and rail operators, to bring in more funds.

In Sussex the flagship project is the Cuckoo Trail, already described in these pages (*see page 31*), which runs from Polegate to Heathfield. Sustrans has also built the much shorter Centurion Way out of Chichester. Both use mainly the tracks of old railway lines.

What Sustrans intends to do is to link these routes with others to provide a viable network, not only in Sussex, but also linking with routes elsewhere. The network map shows routes in Sussex clearly connected to those in Surrey, Kent and Hampshire.

The Cuckoo Trail is already being extended southwards down to Eastbourne where it will connect with the South Coast Cycleway all the way from Dover to Land's End. Some parts of this are already open and well used such as the cycleways along the prom at Brighton, Worthing and Hastings. Others are proving more problematical, among

The Sustrans Good Cycling Code

On all routes:
• Please be courteous!
Always cycle with respect for others, whether other cyclists, pedestrians, people in wheelchairs, horse riders or drivers, and acknowlede those who give way to you.

On shared use paths:
• give way to pedestrians, leaving them plenty of room
• keep to your side of any dividing line
• be prepared to slow down or stop if necessary
• don't expect to cycle at high speeds
• be careful at junctions, bends and entrances
• remember that many people are hard of hearing or visually impaired - don't assume they can see or hear you
• carry a bell and use it - don't surprise people
• give way where there are wheelchair users and horse riders

On roads:
• always follow the Highway Code
• be seen - most accidents to cyclists happen at junctions
• consider wearing a helmet and conspicuous clothing

"Thank you for choosing this environmentally friendly form of transport"

• keep your bike roadworthy
• don't cycle on pavements except where designated - pavements are for pedestrians
• use your bell - not all pedestrians can see you.

In the countryside:
• follow the Country Code
• respect other land management activities such as farming or forestry, and take litter home
• keep erosion to a minimum if offroad
• be self-sufficient - in remote areas carry food, repair kit, map and waterproofs
• try to cycle or use public transport to travel to and from the start and finish of your ride
• cycle within your capabilities
• match your speed to the surface and your skills

them the provision of a route in Seaford, where some of the locals appear to regard cyclists as a form of alien invasion.

Northwards the Cuckoo Trail will eventually meet with those two excellent east-west routes, the Worth Way and the Forest Way, to be part of another route from Canterbury to Gatwick. The Centurion Way will eventually connect Chichester to the South Downs Way while southwards there is already a route from Chichester to Bognor.

Some other parts of the country, thanks to Sustrans or to enlightened councils, have already developed a far more extensive system of routes than those we have in Sussex. Peterborough and Stevenage, to name but two, are fine examples of municipalities that 'think bike', while in York Sustrans has made full use of old railway tracks to provide several long and picturesque routes out of the city. Sustrans will gladly give callers details of routes elsewhere should you be thinking of travelling.

Sustrans is also working with many councils, including some in Sussex, on the Safe Routes to School campaign which provides attractive journeys for youngsters.

The London to Brighton Bike Ride

*T*owards the end of June every year up to 30,000 people, ranging from the superbly fit to the not very fit at all, jump on their bikes and in a collective fit of charitable madness pedal all the way from London to Brighton.

This amazing event is one of the largest participation events anywhere in Britain, and is well worth signing up for

if you relish a cycling challenge – with the additional benefit of raising millions of pounds for the British Heart Foundation in sponsorship.

Most cycle shops will have details of the event from November onwards. Although

At Ditchling, with the arduous ascent of the Beacon yet to come.

there is nothing to stop you simply joining in without entering, this is really against the spirit of an extremely well-organised event which is already bursting at the seams.

It all started with fewer than 30 cyclists riding from Hyde Park to Madeira Drive in Brighton back in 1976. It quickly grew, and a few years ago the start point was moved to Clapham Common, a better meeting place that also avoids riders having to go through central London.

The route is well designed to avoid most main roads. In Sussex it passes through Turners Hill, Ardingly, Wivelsfield Green and Ditchling before the great climb up the Beacon and the lovely glide all the way down to the seafront.

There is a real carnival atmosphere about the ride which really is a celebration of cycling. It is not a race although a few maniacs at the front take it at speed, sometimes cycling back as well. There is plenty of entertainment on the way and refreshments are everywhere, both at special pit stops and at enterprising pubs and cafes along the route.

Getting there can be awkward, but you can either use a spare van or go up on one of the special trains which rail operators put on for the occasion. The ride itself can be annoyingly slow, too, because (to allow for the numbers), riders are often let off at the start in batches of several hundreds in order to go through junctions.

But this is a special event, and the fun outweighs the disadvantages. It's certainly worth trying once, and some people find it so addictive that they do it every year.

There are several other regular rides although none as large. One gaining popularity is held each July from Hampton Court to Hove, with the last stretch over Devil's Dyke. There are several others along long-distance cycle-ways such as the South Downs Way and the Downs Link. Again, your local cycle shop should have details.

The ride finishes at Madeira Drive, watched by huge crowds.

Riding abroad

Sussex is so near to Continental Europe that it is easy to slip across to countries which are much more bike friendly than Britain. The nearest one by far is France.

Fortunately the Newhaven to Dieppe fast ferry takes bikes free of charge when it operates during the summer season. Dieppe is the best of the Channel ports with a good selection of restaurants and a great atmosphere. While the town itself is not built for bikes, you have only to travel a few miles and you can be in the most delightful tranquil countryside.

It can be hilly, especially around the coast, but there are flat exits along the river valleys to the south. Details of cycle routes are available from the tourist information centre in Dieppe.

Ferries from Portsmouth to Caen, Cherbourg and St Malo, where the cycling is also excellent, take bikes too and they can always be put on the backs of cars or vans.

There are two exciting initiatives currently under way:

The English Channel Coastal Cycle Route
The aim is to promote cycling and tourism through the building and promotion of a transfrontier cycle route linking England and France, and also to produce information on the services and facilities available along the way.

In England the route will follow the National Cycle Network between Newhaven and Dover, linking to France via the ferry services to Dieppe and Calais. On the French side a parallel route will be developed along the north French coast between the ports. It's planned that the route will extend to Le Havre and Portsmouth and will also connect to the European cycle network, Eurovélo.

London to Paris Greenway
This project, which involves East Sussex County Council and its French partners, is planned eventually to provide a traffic-free route between the two capitals via the Newhaven-Dieppe ferry.

Unfortunately Eurostar, which offers a quick route to Paris, Brussels and beyond, doesn't take bikes except for the folding variety. It is, though, so cheap and easy to hire bikes in countries such as Holland, Belgium and Germany that you don't actually need to take your own trusty steed abroad with you.

Holland

An attractive option is to begin your continental cycling holiday by taking the Dover-Ostend ferry and riding from Belgium into Holland – the most bike-friendly country anywhere, with hundreds of cycle tracks and routes, some of them miraculously taking you into the centre of large towns without forcing you to share the road with motor vehicles.

The countryside is largely flat, and the few hills that do exist are nothing compared with what we have in Sussex, but don't let that fool you into planning to cover many more miles a day than you'd normally feel comfortable with. True, you don't have the hills to climb, but neither do you have those exhilarating free-wheeling moments coming down the other side: be prepared for more of a steady plod.

Note, too, that the Dutch ride about on sturdy bikes whose thick tyres can cope happily with pine needles and other relatively insignificant sharp objects. In country areas a thin racing tyre is prone to suffer recurrent punctures, so do adapt to the conditions if you have a choice of bikes.

The Isle of Wight

While it is not abroad at all, the Isle of Wight feels like another world, albeit one left in the Sixties, but it so good for cyclists it should be mentioned even in a book about Sussex. Trains take you directly to Portsmouth Harbour from most parts of Sussex. The ferries to Fishbourne and the catamaran to Ryde carry bikes free.

The island itself is made for bikes. As it measures only 22 miles by 12, no journeys are long, yet you can find mile after mile of quiet roads. Teashops, cafes and pubs are never more than a short distance from even the most peaceful spot.

"We may happily potter about the familiar byways of Sussex for ever, but a little investigation opens up new routes, new possibilities"

Useful contacts

Local authorities

The two county councils and Brighton and Hove City Council (*see pages 102–103*) are the only authorities that have responsibility for non-trunk road traffic, including bikes, and they tend to have the most information about cycling, with a wide range of free leaflets available.

These local authorities undertake a range of initiatives, including the construction of new cycle routes and, in East Sussex, a programme of guided rides.

Most of the district and borough councils also produce leaflets about cycling, and they encourage it as a pastime.

Telephone numbers for the councils are:

East Sussex County Council 01273 481000
       Cuckoo Trail ranger 01273 481637
       Forest Way ranger 01273 482670
       Rye Countryside Office 01797 226488
West Sussex County Council 01243 777161
Brighton and Hove City Council 01273 29000
Adur District Council 01273 455566
Arun District Council 01903 737500
Chichester District Council 01243 785166
Crawley Borough Council 01293 438000
Eastbourne Borough Council 01323 415250
Hastings Borough Council 01424 781066
Horsham District Council 01403 215100
Lewes District Council 01273 471600
Mid Sussex District Council 01444 458166
Rother District Council 01424 787500
Wealden District Council 01892 602561
Worthing Borough Council 01903 239999

"East Sussex County Council recognises that cycling is fun, has little effect on the environment, improves fitness and can be quicker than the motor

car for local journeys, but that many potential cyclists are discouraged by danger and pollution caused by traffic. It is therefore committed to improving conditions for cyclists to make cycling safer, convenient and more attractive."

01273 482111 Cycling strategy, cycle route development and the National Cycle Network

01273 481654 Cycling in the countryside, guided rides, cycling leaflets

"West Sussex already has a level of cycling higher than average, yet there is a great potential for increase which has to date been held back by the dominance of motor traffic on the roads. This includes use of cycles for journeys including commuting, shopping and education, as well as leisure and recreation. West Sussex County Council is working to make cycling and walking more attractive and safer for everyone in order to gain the benefits of reduced congestion, pollution and noise, along with increased health and road safety, that wider cycling could bring."

01243 777161 Cycling policy

TRAVEL WISE ®

The publishers are grateful to East Sussex County Council, West Sussex County Council and Brighton & Hove City Council for sponsorship which has allowed the production of quality maps throughout *Cycling Sussex*. On these pages we give brief 'mission statements' from each of the three local authorities, which jointly promote 'green travelling' through their TRAVELWISE initiative.

"Brighton & Hove City Council is encouraging cycling as part of its sustainable transport strategy which aims to make Brighton & Hove a vibrant and healthy, people-friendly city in which to live and travel. More cycle routes are being created to make cycling more attractive, more cycle stands are being installed for secure parking and the council also teaches cycling in schools."

01273 292475 Urban and general issues

01273 292383 Bridleways and rural routes; guided cycle rides

01273 292258 Safer routes to schools and cycle training

Or go to the council's website and click on 'Transport': www.brighton-hove.gov.uk

Sustrans
This splendid organisation (*see page 93*) gains much of its income from members.
  National information 0117 929 0888.
  Website www.sustrans.org.uk
  South East office 01273 624426
        (145 Islingword Road, Brighton)

Other cycling organisations
Typical of the Sussex organisations dedicated to improving conditions for riders is **Bricycles**, the Brighton Hove and District Cycling Campaign. This not only pioneered the cycle lane along Hove seafront but also has a vigorous social section including rides both in Britain and abroad.
Bricycles website: www.fpipes.freeserve.co.uk/bricyles.html

  The largest and oldest cycling organisation in the UK is the **CTC** or **Cyclists' Touring Club**. It has 70,000 members and local organisations in most big towns. The CTC provides help to cyclists and provides third party insurance and legal aid free to all members. Its phone number is 01483 417217.

  Cycle Lewes, as its name implies, concentrates on a rather smaller area of the county. Website: cyclelewes.cjb.net.

Bikes on trains

*I*t's easy if you're going on a walk to reach a distant starting point by bus or car, but with cycling the problem of getting there is often the bike itself.

Most riders won't want to undertake a ride of 30 miles, often on busy roads, to and from the start of a tranquil saunter through leafy lanes in the countryside. Even if you are able to carry your bike (or bikes) on the car, a growing awareness of pollution and congestion makes leaving the vehicle at home a more desirable option – and often the train is the best answer.

Old-fashioned trains, such as those rapidly being phased out on the East and West Coastway lines, have guard's vans which can take a number of bikes, often up to ten. There is seldom any problem about this except when the vans are also full of cyclists en masse, people in wheelchairs or parents with buggies. Newer trains have less space, but are able to take two or three bicycles in specially marked portions of the train.

During the morning and evening rush hours, no bikes at all are allowed on trains going into and out of London. Folding bikes can be carried on any train.

The Gatwick Express has plenty of room for bikes and no restrictions on when they can be carried. Thameslink allows bikes between Brighton and Gatwick.

New trains are being introduced during the next few years on most lines in Sussex. It is unclear at the moment how many bikes they will be able to take, but space will be available for some at least.

Most large stations have places where bikes can be left locked up and reasonably secure, and at Brighton – by far the busiest station – they can be left under cover.

Weekend engineering works can be a pain and a bore. Not only do they extend journey times greatly but they also have replacement buses for sections of the line and bikes can't be carried on them.

It's always best to check well in advance when work is

being carried out (summer months are usually free of major engineering works), and details are available at most stations for a month or two ahead. A leaflet called *Cycling by Train* is published each year, covering the whole country.

The good thing about taking bikes by trains is that in this part of the world they are carried free of charge. Most guards are usually helpful about bikes. They will open doors for you and even carry bikes out.

It is worth travelling off peak for good savings. A Network card covers the whole of the South East and gives savings of a third on most journeys. Family Railcards cover the whole country, but the discounts are less good than they used to be. Note, however, that the rules changed in May 2001, when Thameslink began to charge a flat £1 for accompanied children (off peak), even without a Network card.

There are also student and pensioner railcards which give good savings and which are well worth buying for any regular travellers entitled to them.

With Connex services being transferred to Govia, the company which already runs the ThamesLink services, the local rail network in our area is due to be restyled the New Southern Railway. What this will mean for cyclists isn't yet certain, but the chief executive, Keith Ludeman, has said that cycling will be 'a key issue' for the company.

Govia has committed itself to improving secure cycle provision at stations and says that it will provide flexible space on new trains, which could provide capacity for up to eight bicycles.

Although the policy will be reviewed from time to time, the company says that it has no plans for a reservation system or to impose charges for cycles.

Cycle shops

Cycle shops come in all shapes and sizes. The large ones often (but not always) have the advantage on price through bulk buying, but they seldom offer much expertise. Specialist stores will always give you advice on what bike is best suited for your needs and will usually let you have a trial run so that you can judge for yourself.

They generally offer a repairs service which is useful for the average rider who lacks much mechanical knowledge. Most of them also offer regular six monthly checks – useful if you want to keep a new bike in sparkling condition.

Good cycle dealers are worth their weight in ball bearings. They can usually judge your needs accurately and cater for them expertly. I have used the same one in Hove for more than 30 years and regard the proprietors as friends.

A selection of Sussex cycle shops:

BRACKLESHAM BAY
The Cycle Shop, 4c Azara Parade, Bracklesham Bay, Chichester, West Sussex PO20 8HP 01243 672601

FOREST ROW
Future Cycles, Lower Square, Forest Row, East Sussex RH18 5HD 01342 822847

HOVE
Webbs Cycles, 91 Boundary Road, Hove, East Sussex BN3 7GA 01273 417658

LEWES
Twoplustwo, 31 Western Road, Lewes, East Sussex BN7 1RL 01273 480479

WORTHING
Michael's Cycles, 21 South Farm Road, Worthing, West Sussex BN14 7AD 01903 232884

About the author

Born in 1942, Adam Trimingham has been cycling since he was knee high to an Elswick-Hopper, and he still covers 3,000 miles a year on his sturdy steed.

He is married, with four children and two bikes. He also has a tandem, a trailer and the second-hand bike that his parents gave him when he was six. He writes for the *Argus* newspaper in Brighton and rides to work every day.

Adam's first book, *Trimingham's Brighton*, (published by Pomegranate Press at £6.50) paints an affectionate portrait of our city by the sea, drawing on his 30 years' experience as a local reporter. There are fascinating stories on every page, and characters galore.

Index of places

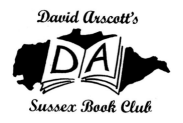

David Arscott's

Sussex Book Club

The home of books about Sussex

So many books are written about Sussex that it's difficult to keep track of them all.

No longer! Writer/publisher David Arscott has formed a lively book club which will keep you abreast of everything's that's being written and give you the opportunity to select from a wide range of new titles.

This is a rare no-catches book club:
- Membership is completely free
- There's no obligation to buy
- You won't be sent books you haven't asked for
- Any books you order will be sent to you completely free of post & packing charges

To enrol in this growing fraternity of Sussex book lovers simply send your name and address to:

The Sussex Book Club
Dolphin House
51 St Nicholas Lane
Lewes, Sussex BN7 2JZ

or email:
sussexbooks@compuserve.com